I Hate Meetings

Also By the Author:

Advertising Layout and Art Direction
Visual Persuasion: Effect of Pictures on the Subconscious
An Art Director's Viewpoint
How to Live with a Neurotic Dog
How to Live with a Neurotic Wife
How to Look Like Somebody in Business Without Being Anybody
How to Play Golf in the Low 120's
How to Live with a Neurotic Husband
How to Be Analyzed by a Neurotic Psychoanalyst
How to Get a Job Without Asking for It
Systematic Approach to Advertising Creativity
Games Dogs Play
New York Driver's Instant Map Guide
500 Names for Cats
How to Live with a Neurotic Cat
My Cat—the First Twenty Years

I Hate Meetings

STEPHEN BAKER

with drawings by
New Yorker magazine cartoonist
Arnie Levin

Macmillan Publishing Company
New York
Collier Macmillan Publishers
London

Copyright © 1983 by Stephen Baker
Copyright © 1983 by Arnie Levin

All rights reserved. No part of this book may be reproduced or transmitted in any form or by any means, electronic or mechanical, including photocopying, recording or by any information storage and retrieval system, without permission in writing from the Publisher.

Macmillan Publishing Company
866 Third Avenue, New York, N.Y. 10022
Collier Macmillan Canada, Inc.

Library of Congress Cataloging in Publication Data
Baker, Stephen, 1921–
　I hate meetings.
　1. Meetings—Anecdotes, facetiae, satire, etc.
I. Title.
PN6231.M42B34　1983　　　658.4'563'0207　　　83-16189
ISBN 0-02-506370-7

10 9 8 7 6 5 4 3 2 1

Printed in the United States of America

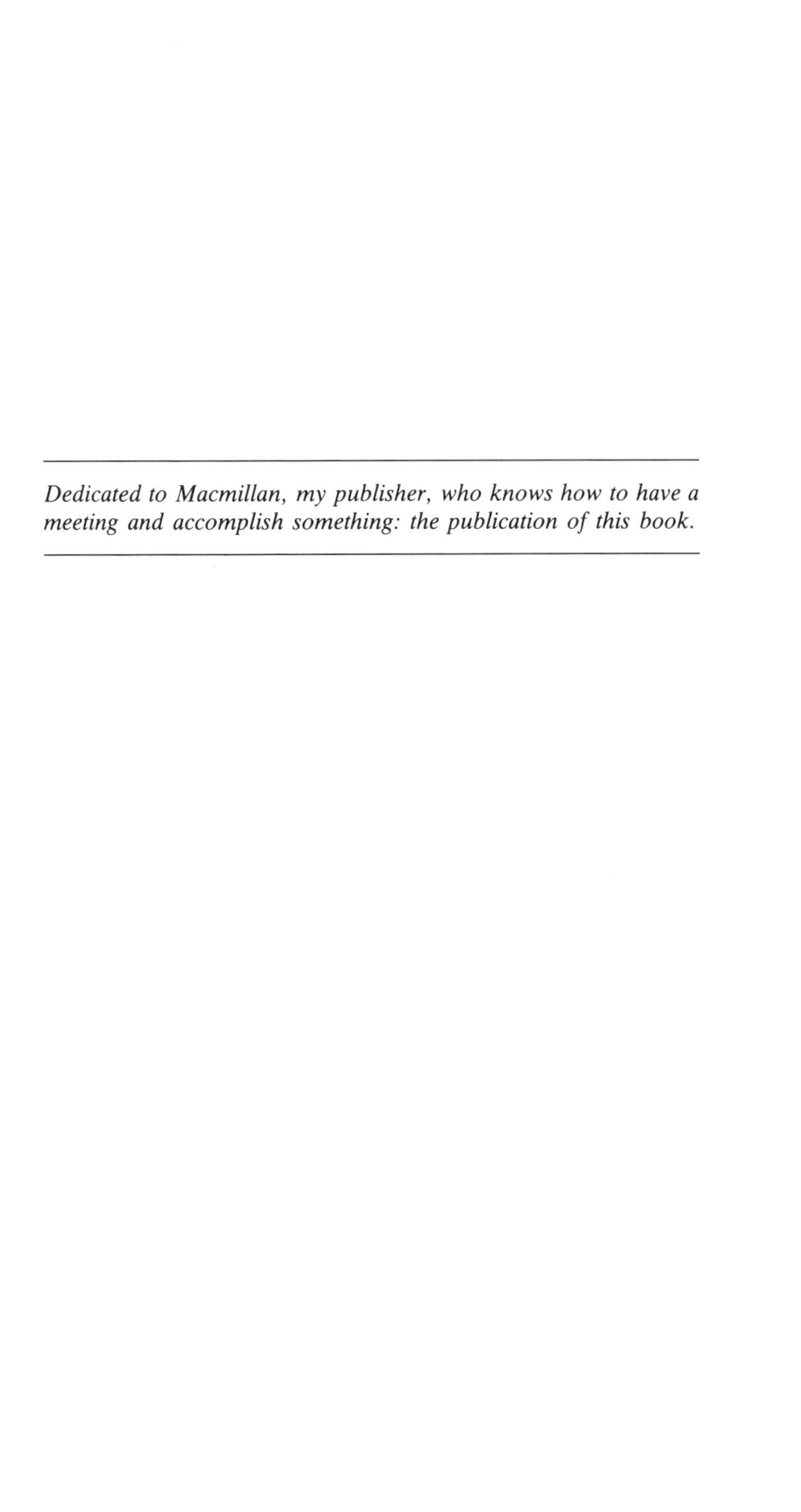

Dedicated to Macmillan, my publisher, who knows how to have a meeting and accomplish something: the publication of this book.

Contents

Chapter 1:	If meetings accomplish nothing, why have them at all?	2
Chapter 2:	How to attend a meeting and catch up on your sleep at the same time	14
Chapter 3:	How to look like an authority even when you're not	18
Chapter 4:	What to say when you have nothing on your mind	24
Chapter 5:	What to do when you don't understand the situation	38
Chapter 6:	Creating the right atmosphere	54
Chapter 7:	How to act organized even if you're not	64
Chapter 8:	What every chairperson should know about problem people around the conference table	74
Chapter 9:	How to keep from making a decision	82
Chapter 10:	How to meet for business outside the office and accomplish absolutely nothing	96
Appendix:	The effective chairperson's quiz	110

I Hate Meetings

CHAPTER ONE

If meetings accomplish nothing, why have them at all?

A LOT OF PEOPLE ASK: Why have meetings? This is a good question and one that certainly deserves your attention before your next meeting.

Meetings, of course, do serve a purpose. Consider this: Our national economy is based on a 35- to 45-hour work week. Without meetings this figure would dwindle to a few hours at the most. Our whole system, as we know it, would collapse.

It is natural to want to gather 'round; baboons and penguins have been doing it for years. But credit for refining the technique goes to *Homo sapiens*. **They are the ones who invented the chair, the tabletop, and the conference room, making it possible to have meetings from morning to late afternoon five days a week.**

The advantages of having matters resolved by a group have long been obvious to those who work—or pretend to work—in industry and commerce. Meetings satisfy deep-seated psychological needs and, as such, cannot be dismissed as mere frivolity. To wit, meetings provide opportunities for:

- The consumption of large quantities of coffee and doughnuts, at company expense

- Saying hello to colleagues you haven't seen since yesterday's meeting
- Telling jokes
- Horseplay
- Making speeches
- Looking important
- Making others look unimportant
- Getting away from the desk
- Posing as a leader
- Displaying expertise on subjects you know nothing about and/or inventing new words
- Taking a rest
- Telling someone he or she has a mental block
- Complaining (about lack of organization, poor management, underpay, too many meetings, etc.)
- Listening to other people's ideas you can take credit for in the future
- Spreading responsibilities around

The last point is especially important, and is itself reason enough to hold a meeting. Those in top management know only too well that it is better to have several people sharing the same responsibility than to have it placed in the lap of one individual. ***The latter approach would lead to the eventual dismissal of <u>everyone</u> in the company, including the president.***

The ability to assign tasks in such a way that no one is sure what exactly he or she is supposed to do has long been considered the mark of a true executive. It is usually referred to as Ability to Delegate Responsibility. It is the essence of running a corporation, for it guarantees enough problems to keep everyone busy for a long time. Moreover, the procedure allows the delegator to spend more time on the golf course and refine his putting technique.

| FIRST MEETING | SECOND MEETING |

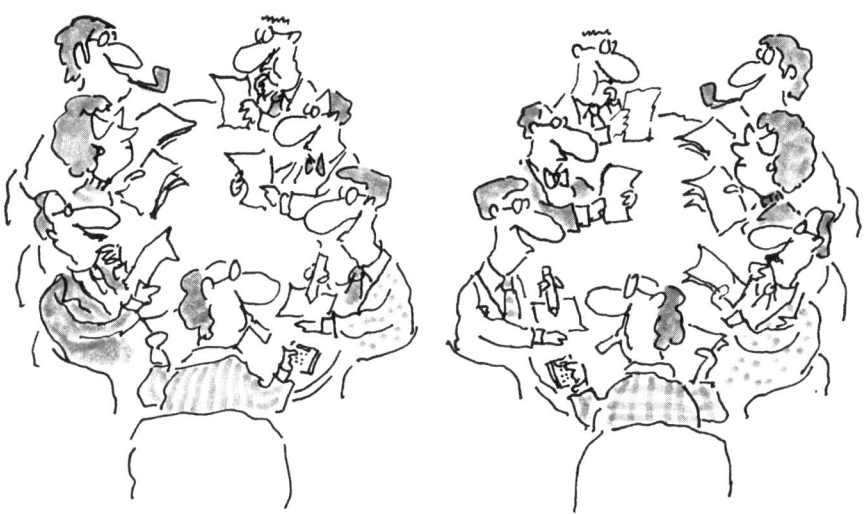

People like to point out that little, if anything, is accomplished at meetings. They are missing the point altogether. The main purpose of having a meeting is to find an excuse for having another one soon thereafter, preferably on the same topic.

THE AMOUNT of confusion a meeting generates is in direct proportion to the number of people who attend. The larger the assemblage, the better the chances for confusion. Meetings attended only by those who should be there do not last long enough, and too often they could just as well be held in an executive washroom stall.

In passing responsibilities, it is important to know where to place the blame if anything goes wrong, which is almost always the case. A good rule to remember is that responsibility should always flow <u>away</u>, not <u>toward</u> the delegator. This is known as the <u>One-Way Rule</u>, and it is scrupulously followed by all successful executives.

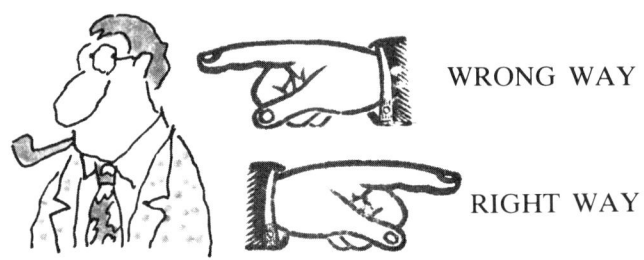

WRONG WAY

RIGHT WAY

The best person at whom to wave an accusing finger is the one at the bottom of the organizational chart. Identifying the culprit as someone in a higher position than you (your boss, for instance) is not only considered poor manners, but an act of stupidity. Unless you have your resumé handy, it is a risk hardly worth taking.

CHAIRMAN OF THE BOARD

PRESIDENT

EXECUTIVE VICE PRESIDENT

SECRETARY & TREASURER

MARKETING DIRECTOR

SALES MANAGER

GENERAL MANAGER

ADVERTISING DIRECTOR

PURCHASING DIRECTOR

STOCKROOM CLERK

Only your imagination limits you in identifying a person as solely responsible for your deeds. Take the mailroom clerk for example. More likely than not he will not be at the meeting to defend himself. And even if he is, he will have no idea what you're talking about. Singling him out also offers the opportunity to show the human side of your nature, your unabiding compassion for the underdog—another sign that you are Managerial Material, tough but tender. The following phrases in referring to the perpetrator will stand you in good stead:

"The poor devil."

"He's too young to know better."

"I still like him as a person."

"We all make mistakes."

"To err is human."

"For chrissakes, he's only a mailroom clerk!"

Now flash your best smile. Others at the conference table will take their cue and the spirit of forgiveness will prevail once again. With the next item looming large on the agenda, the matter will be quickly dropped to everyone's relief—especially those who are beginning to feel guilty about their own mistakes too.

If there's no mailroom clerk, try *in absentia* the cleaning lady who only comes in at night.

HANDY ALIBIS FOR NOT GETTING THE JOB DONE

My grandmother had to be taken to the hospital
My grandmother had to be brought home from the hospital
Had to go to my son's graduation ceremonies
Had to go to my son's wedding
Had to go to court to bail my son out of jail
My secretary is on vacation/jury duty/has a cold
The accountant is on vacation/jury duty/has a cold
I just came back from vacation/jury duty/had a cold
My secretary is new on the job
The company car wasn't available
Doesn't meet my standards

SCAPEGOATS TO BLAME ANYTHING ON

President of the United States
U.S. Senate
U.S. Congress
The Republican Party
The Democratic Party
Liberals
Conservatives
Communists
Internal Revenue Service
U.N. Ambassador
National Security Adviser
Government subsidies
The Middle East
Inflation
MX missile system
Federal spending
High interest rates
Lack of capital
Foreign import
Nuclear warheads
Bureaucracy
U.S. Post Office
Diplomatic immunity
Crime
The weather

Nuclear freeze
Antinuclear protesters
Toxic substances
Overzealous environmentalists
Long Island Railroad
Plumbers
Garbage collectors
Automobile mechanics
Traffic conditions
Public utility companies
Airline schedules
Violence on television
Landlords
Tenants
Richard Nixon
Playboy
National Inquirer
Smoking
Aching back
Tennis elbow
Poor golf grip
Illegible handwriting
People who don't return phone calls

ABOVE REPROACH

Walt Disney
Norman Rockwell
George Washington
Ludwig van Beethoven
Queen of England
The Pope
American astronauts
American Indians
Microsurgeons
Anthropologists
Rolls-Royce engine

Ford Foundation
Pregnant women
Children under six
Second medical opinions
The New York Times
Spelling-bee winners
Black college graduates
Brewer's yeast
Good weather
Santa Claus

Johnny Carson
Ed McMahon
Lee Iacocca
Alice (from Wonderland)
Christmas
IBM
Goodyear Blimp
Oxford English Dictionary
God

How to Have a BIG Meeting and Accomplish Absolutely Nothing

Big meetings are the most fun of all. With so many people attending, progress comes to a near standstill.

How to Shift the Emphasis on TEAMWORK—and Away from Yourself

NEVER SAY	SAY
My responsibility . . .	In our opinion . . .
My . . .	Corporate policy demands . . .
The buck stops at my desk	The buck stops at the conference table
I'm against it	We're all against it . . .
To my way of thinking . . .	After much thought . . .
It has been my policy . . .	It's standard operating procedure . . .
I recommend it	Far be it for me to make a recommendation but . . .
I will approve it	Subject to everyone's approval
Let me decide	Let's put democracy to work

Every Meeting Must Have a Leader

He or she may go under the name of Chairperson, Manager, Ranking Executive, CEO (Chief Executive Officer), or, simply and most often, as That Bum. The final outcome of the meeting hinges on this person's commanding performance. His or her responsibilities run the gamut. All are important. To mention just a few:

- To make sure the coffee is hot
- To see that everyone has a chair
- To see that he or she has a chair, too
- To stretch the meeting out—all day long, if at all possible but never past 5 P.M.
- To make sure everyone has a good time

The last point is especially important. It comes under the heading of Keeping Up Employee Morale.

People often wonder why oval-shaped conference tables enjoy such universal popularity. The truth is they haven't always. It took years of experimentation to arrive at today's shape.

First there was the Rectangular Table with the chairperson at one end as the focus of attention. The implication of this arrangement was clear: Responsibility for conducting the meeting rested with the person at the head. But not everyone liked this idea.

The Circular Table was designed to do away with the one-person rule. However, this shape brought with it a whole new set of problems. Now anyone could lay claim to sitting at the head of the table and thus being in charge.

The Oval Table was finally arrived at as a compromise. It grew in size as businesses hired more people who didn't quite know what to do with their time and insisted on meeting. A highly polished mahogany or teak finish was added later for making attendees feel more important.

CHAPTER TWO

How to attend a meeting and catch up on your sleep at the same time

MORE AND MORE PEOPLE are discovering that the conference room is as good a place as any to take a nap, perhaps even better than the bedroom at home. Conditions are perfect, particularly when a presentation is being made. The soothing quality of a voice running off facts and figures has often been compared to that of a mother's lullaby.

While most corporations do not take kindly to employees' suggestions that recliners or rockers should be part of the decor in a conference room—and flatly refuse to supply hammocks, mattresses, and waterbeds for those looking for maximum creature comforts—basic office furniture pretty much serves the same purpose. There are chairs complete with armrests, seat cushions, and padded backrests, and the table is so designed that the legroom far exceeds that found in movie theaters, at bars, or the back of taxicabs—not to mention the tourist class seats on a Boeing 727.

During a meeting you may close your eyes without attracting undue attention. ***Your comatose state will be interpreted as your being immersed in thought. In any case, closed eyes are preferable to glazed eyes.***

You will have a problem only if you:

- Sleep through the *entire* meeting
- Snore (and wake up others)
- Slip off your chair and onto the floor
- Slump forward and whack your head on the table

It really doesn't matter if you are in the habit of talking in your sleep. **Nobody will notice the difference between the comments you make in your sleep and wakeful moments. Nor should you be concerned about being a somnambulist. Should you grope your way toward the door, people will think you're heading for the washroom.**

If you are the chairperson presiding over the meeting, you must, of course, guard against losing the appearance of being in charge. Try one of the following when you feel you are no longer able to fight off sleep:

Wear dark glasses.

Cover your face with your hands as if reflecting on a problem.

Lean back in your chair and gaze at the ceiling so no one can see your face.

You may choose to stay awake for long periods of time, if only to impress your audience. ***Admittedly, this requires a great deal of self-discipline. Still, it may be worth a try on a special occasion.*** Here are some useful tips:

- Pinch yourself
- Ask someone to pinch you every fifteen minutes
- Stretch out your arms and take a deep breath
- Make faces at the chairperson
- Talk to your neighbor or, better still, someone far across the table
- Hum your favorite song
- Have something to eat (perhaps the pastrami sandwich with dill pickles you brought along to the meeting)
- Ask a question even if you don't have any
- Excuse yourself, go outside, and jog around the block

There also may be times when you simply cannot fall asleep. Perhaps it is still early in the day, or you have just come from another meeting where you have already caught up on your sleep. Still, you don't want to waste your time and lose out on your chance to get some rest. Try this:

- Take a sleeping pill
- Slowly rock back and forth in your chair
- Fix your gaze on a spot on the ceiling
- Lie down on the floor

CHAPTER THREE

How to look like an authority even when you're not

T HERE WILL BE TIMES when it will behoove you to look important, holding this pose for perhaps several minutes at a time. This might be the case, if you are chairing the meeting.

The best way to create an impression of omniscience is not by talking but by listening. Listening beats talking every way. ***Without saying a word, you can still convey the idea that you have information not readily available to just anybody.***

"He's a good listener" ranks high among the compliments bestowed on a leader. It suggests that you are one of that rare species who, through self-control, has learned to keep his mouth shut regardless of his position in the company. Your silence will not only inspire respect among your peers, but more importantly, it will save you from making a complete fool of yourself.

Your pregnant pauses will be interpreted as a sign of character. Rising above the day-to-day petty concerns that beset the rank and file, your mind is thought to travel in the highest of corporate orbits. Everyone understands that you, as a top executive, should be allowed to let his imagination roam free, to focus in on the Big Picture with the Bottom Line in mind.

All great ideas begin with a gleam in the eye.

The more preoccupied you appear, the more respect you will gain. Practice the art in front of the mirror every morning before going to the office. Loosen up those jaws. Wrinkle that nose; raise those eyebrows.

Research shows that body language and facial expression play as important a part in conveying a message as do words. Sometimes even more so. Not everyone understands English but everyone with a pair of eyes is able to see. This is a fortunate circumstance for any chairperson who wisely chooses to remain silent when he or she has nothing to say.

On Becoming a Good Listener

Here is how to make your audience think you're paying close attention.

Cup your ears. *Frown.* *Rub your eyes as if you're seeing the light for the first time.*

Wink as if you understood perfectly.

Raise an eyebrow. If you have the energy, raise them both.

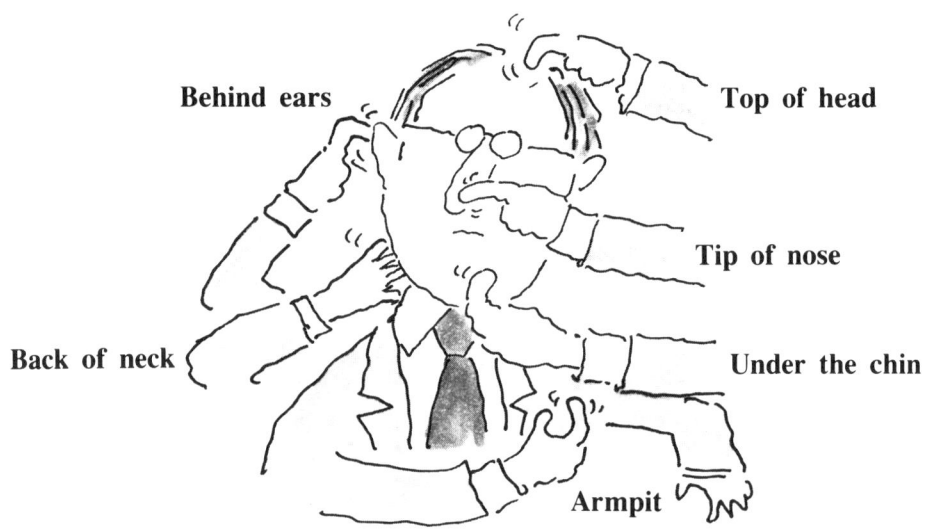

When in doubt, scratch. All top executives do.

Tilt your head.   *Smile knowingly.*   *Listen with open-mouthed amazement.*

What Every Executive Should Know About Executive Posture

Cross your arms.

Lean forward and support your chin in your hands.

Lean back and clasp your hands behind your head.

*But don't lean back **too** far.*

… CHAPTER FOUR

What to say when you have nothing on your mind

IT IS IMPORTANT that you make yourself heard at meetings, even if it means sacrificing your sleeping schedule. This is known as Making Your Presence Felt.

If at all possible, use words to express what appears to be an opinion. Grunts, snorts, squeaks, squawks, or the sound of a stifled yawn probably won't do. Nor will booing, blowing your nose, banging your shoe on the table, or tossing empty beer cans across the room into a wastebasket.

Try, if you can, to string words together to form a sentence; the longer and more complex the better. There is always a chance that your listeners will lose track of what you're saying before you finish your statement, and will therefore not be able to hold it against you at the next meeting.

There will be times, of course, when you will have nothing at all to say. That should not deter you from posing as an authority figure. ***In fact, it is precisely at such times that you should give full vent to your oratory powers.***

You are expected to have opinions. It matters not a bit whether they have relevance to the issue or not. Talking for the sake of talking is an accepted practice at meetings, and no one will think the worse for it. If attendees addressed themselves only to a meeting's relevant issues, then the silence at the meeting would be deadening.

When in doubt, mumble. Speak in a low voice, between your teeth, from the side of your mouth, or through your nose. Here is an ideal pose.

Allow a few noncommittal words to escape your lips, such as "and," "because," or, for a show of excitement, "God forbid!" Your audience will take comfort in the fact that you are able to make sounds, such as they may be.

An alternative to mumbling is to go to the opposite extreme and shout at the top of your lungs. This is known as Making a Speech. The advantage of Making a Speech is that your delivery will so intrigue your audience that they will stop paying attention to the points you're making. ***The less important your message, the louder your voice should be.*** Project. Use your diaphragm. It's safer than using your brain. Politicians have been using their diaphragms for years and with great success.

One of the hallmarks of an accomplished orator is the ability to show emotions. This is of paramount importance. ***It matters little what the words are as long as they come from the heart, or better still, from the depths of your heart.***

Laugh.   *Cry.*

Pound on the table.

Break the visual monotony. Pace back and forth. (But do not walk out the door.)

Flail your arms.

Throw off your jacket.

Roll up your shirtsleeves.

Rise to the occasion.

There is no reason why you should ever run out of words. The English language is rich in vocabulary. It offers members of the business establishment an opportunity to use many words instead of one. Study and master how this is done, and you will have taken another giant step up the corporate ladder.

DON'T SAY	SAY
I agree	I most certainly agree We share the same opinion I'm with you all the way We're on the same wavelength You've got something there Now you're talking
I don't agree	I beg to differ with you I take issue with that I take exception to that I'm not sure if I follow you
Yes	Yes indeed By all means Right on Yes sirree You bet your life Yes, yes, yes, yes
No	Not quite It can't be Have you considered the possibility . . . Not by a long shot No, no, no, NO
Unacceptable	Oh, how I wish we could do it The only problem . . . Not at this point in time I admire your enthusiasm but . . .
Acceptable	Good idea I put my John Hancock on it It's a thought Why didn't I think of that?

Adding a few words to every sentence may seem insignificant at first. *But they add up, and you will eventually master the fine art of talking at length about nothing.*

Always include the name of the individual to whom you are speaking when you answer a question. This will not only make the other person feel flattered, but, more important, will help make your sentences longer. Remember, every syllable counts. Avoid one-syllable nicknames; for example, Theodore is preferable to Ted. As are Elizabeth, Jeremiah, Anastopoulos, or Aleksandrenko to their shortened forms.

Some speakers are able to extend considerably their stay on the floor by using both first and last (and middle, if there is one) names when talking to an audience. It takes a long time to stumble over a name like Michael-Guillaume Jean de Crevecoeur, particularly if you choose to repeat it three times before you get it right.

If using full names is too formal for your taste, but you still wish to stretch out the time, simply include everyone's first name after each and every statement.

> **Don't you agree, James, Robert, Paula, Nicholas, Edmond, Sandra, Monica, Grifford, Fergus, Ormond, Josephine, Norman, Gale, Edith, Henrietta, Harold?**

BEFORE MAKING YOUR POINT, spend time working up to it. This is a sure way to get your audience confused right at the start. For instance:

"Ladies and gentlemen. I will get right to the crux of the problem. As you know, I value your time, my time, our time. Time is the most precious commodity we have."

"I will be brief. No beating around the bush. No putting our heads in the sand. Let's get down to the facts. I've always been for brevity. And I'm always for avoiding platitudes."

"Keep it simple and to the point, I always say, so I will keep my message simple and to the point. I believe in simplicity and directness, as opposed to lack of it. Too many of us complicate things, embellish them, draw them out."

"If there's something you don't understand, say so. Speak up. Just raise your hand, stand up, and tell me what's on your mind. On second thought, you don't even have to stand up. After all, this isn't a classroom."

"If there is one thing I hate, it is a long-winded speaker. ... You know, the type who is so enamored with his voice that he just doesn't know when to stop. No sir. He just keeps on and on and on."

"Now I am a man of a few words. I make my point and that's it. I tell you where it's at, where I am coming from, where we are all heading. Briefly. I don't believe in being redundant. Never. That's because I am a man of a few words."

How to Leave a Question Unanswered

Never offend your audience by fending off inquiries. Weigh the questions, evaluate them, show how much you care. Loss for answer should not deter you from giving one anyway.

THE NONDECISION MAKER'S BEST FRIEND: EYEGLASSES

Always have one or more pairs of eyeglasses in your pocket, even if you are blessed with 20/20 vision. Wielding them in your hands will so engage the attention of your listener that he or she will forget the question.

That's a very good question.

Drop the eyeglasses down low on your nose and peer over them.

Glad you brought this to my attention.

Push them up on your forehead and stare hard at your audience.

My sentiments exactly.

Wear them at the top of your head and grin.

> Let me think about this.

Nibble on one ear piece. Then the other.

> A fine idea.

Clean lenses often while you think of an answer.

Hold eyeglasses up against the light to see if they are clean.

Take them off. Put them back on. Repeat.

WHAT TO DO WITH A BRIEFCASE

To prove that you're the type who never leaves his or her work behind, always carry a briefcase—to airports, to restaurants, from one office to another, and most of all, to the executive washroom. At a business meeting this is among the most useful accessories with which to create the right impression. If monogrammed with gold letters, it shows you're getting nearer to the top.

As you take your seat, place your briefcase on the floor beside you with a <u>thud</u>. That's to get attention.

Place the briefcase on the table in front of you with a <u>clatter</u>, snap it open with a sharp <u>click</u>, and examine the insides.

Every once in a while put a memo or two in your briefcase. Do not let anyone see what else is in there: two bottles of bourbon, a chicken-tuna sandwich, a deck of playing cards, toothbrush, a present for your lady-friend.

Ouch!
Lo and behold!
Hello!
Halloo!
Oh!
Bah!
Heaven knows!
Eureka!
Oh, yeah!
Hey!
Over the top!
Well, well!
Bingo!
All's well!
Jumping Jehoshaphat!
Hoity-toity!
Give 'em hell!
Did you ever?
Whee!
Wow!
Mmmmmm
Ooooooo
Man!
Hot dog!
Oo-la-la!

How do you like
 them apples!
Isn't that the limit!
Of all the ...
It shouldn't happen
 to a dog!
Ugh!
Phew!
Phoo!
Boo!
Pay!
Well and good!
So much the better!
The worst is yet to
 come!
Oh, dear!
Ah, me!
Oh, my!
Oh, boy!
Goody, goody!
What a life!
Tsk-tsk!
Good heavens!
Glory be!

Heaven be praised!
Hallelujah!
Gadzooks!
You don't say!
What do you know!
Can such things be?
Will wonders never
 cease!
Can you beat that!
For crying out loud!
Yipes!
All hail!
Hear! hear!
Good!
Aha!
Gosh!
Gee!
Gad!
Doggone!
Damn!
By jove!
Hurray!
Yippee!
Tra-la-la

#$%¢&*!@!

Expletives are for those who feel they have been silent long enough. Use them when someone talks. The louder the better. They too show that you a) are listening and b) you have an opinion.

35

If you're running out of subjects, try sports talk. You have a wide selection of topics from which to pick. Lack of familiarity should not stop you from bringing them up. Using the right terminology will assure your place as an expert.

BASEBALL

Words to use: assist, base stealing, bean ball, bounder, choke, curve ball, floated, force out, foul ball, ground ball, hit the dirt, knocked out of the box, knuckler, meat hand, on deck, pitchout, pull the string, round-the-horn, shake-off, slugger, spit ball, submarine delivery, Texas League, World Series.

BASKETBALL

Words to use: baseball pass, basket hanging, box and one, brush off, dunking, fake, fast break, hook shot, lay-up, live ball, loose man-to-man, pass and cut, recovery, roll, set play.

FOOTBALL

Words to use: area blocking, balanced line, ball is spotted, blitz, broken-field running, bump and run, buttonhook, clipping, dead ball, deep back, double wing, down-and-in, drop back, eat the ball, encroachment, end around, fade back, flag, flanker back, flat pass, free ball, goal to go, ground gainer, hear footsteps, hit the hole, illegal motion, intentional grounding, juke, kill the clock, lateral, long count, loss of a down, offside, peeling travelers, piling on, sack, sealback, secondary, setback, slant, sled, snap, straight arm, tailback, up back wedge.

TENNIS

Words to use: angle games, anticipatory position, Australian formation, backspin, chalk, chop, dead ball, deep-court game, Eastern grip, forcing shot, on the rise, poach, power game, put away, seeding, smash, spin the racket, take the net, topspin, trajectory, Western grip, wood shot.

GOLF

Words to use: bite, break the green, carry, casual water, choke down, cut-up, drop, explosion shot, fat shot, flagstick, a gimme, gross score, holeable, lie, lip, out-of-bounds, provisional ball, push, read the green, selaff, shank, slice, stroke hole, tee shot, three-putt, through the green, up and down, water hazards, yips.

SAILING

Words to use: ballast, bear off, bilge, centerboard, chain plates, chock, cleat, committee boat, cutter rig, dinghy, dipping lug, fun, head to wind, heel, in stays, keel, lateral plane, leeway, luff, lug rig, mainsail, mizzen, national classes, obstruction to sea room, off the wind, on the wind, outhaul, pay out, port tack, proper course, rake, rating, reaching, reeve, stemway, travelers, trim, waterline, windward, yaw.

If discussion still lags, try something more profound. Switch the subject to the weather, your wife and kids, a vacation in the Caribbean, your fixing a flat tire, or installation of a new septic tank.

Tell a good story, if you can remember one. Buy a book and memorize a few for emergencies. But keep them brief, say under forty-five minutes. Always begin with the phrase "Have you heard this one?" Do <u>not</u> wait for the answer but proceed immediately. To tip your audience off to the funny parts, laugh heartily at your own punch lines.

Don't ever take yourself too seriously. ***Nobody else will.***

CHAPTER FIVE

What to do when you don't understand the situation

T HERE WILL BE TIMES when you feel you haven't the slightest idea what is going on. *This is a very common occurrence and one you should not be too concerned about. It has yet to keep any meeting goer from fully and enthusiastically participating in any discussion.*

It bears repeating that what counts is not what you know but what others think you know. If you're an executive aspiring to rise to new heights in the organization, you obviously can no longer confess ignorance of any subject. However, only when you are at the very top can you afford to take such a position. At that point you do not make mistakes anymore; at best, you are ahead of your time, at worst, you are ill-advised.

If you're ever at a loss for words you should shake your head vigorously. It makes no difference whether you shake your head up and down (indicating approval) or side to side (indicating disapproval). Either way, your action suggests that you Have a Point of View.

With moving your head in any direction, of course, goes a certain amount of risk. Out of curiosity someone might ask you to expound on your point of view, for example. If this should happen, you have a number of options at your disposal, some of which have been touched upon earlier. If they do not serve the purpose, you can always fall back on shrugging your shoulders, smile knowingly, and let out a deep and audible sigh.

Show that you understand and that you're open to the opinion of others.

Chances are your audience will be so delighted, if not surprised, at your showing any reaction at all that they will stop bothering you. Should they keep pestering you, don't be afraid to excuse yourself and say that you must heed the call of nature and leave immediately.

ONE OF THE BEST WAYS to look busy is to take notes. For maximum effect, be sure you keep your hands moving—up, down, sideways. The more energetic the movements, the better. Cross out words, sentences, even entire pages with a flourish. Throw the discarded sheets over your shoulder with a wide sweep. Cover the floor with pieces of paper.

Jotting down thoughts on a legal pad is a skill in itself and takes years of dedicated professional practice. The loftier your position in the company, the more elaborate your note-taking should be. Notes taken during meetings of the top executives of some of America's leading corporations show that this is indeed the case.

Notes taken by the chief executive officer of a multinational corporation during a stockholders meeting.

Notes taken by a general manager of a large oil company during a senate subcommittee investigation.

3/21/84
10:30 PM

JOE
is
a

SO IS
BOB
ARNOLD
JUDITH
MORT
JONATHAN
etc. etc. etc

Notes taken by the president of a bank during a conference of the board of directors.

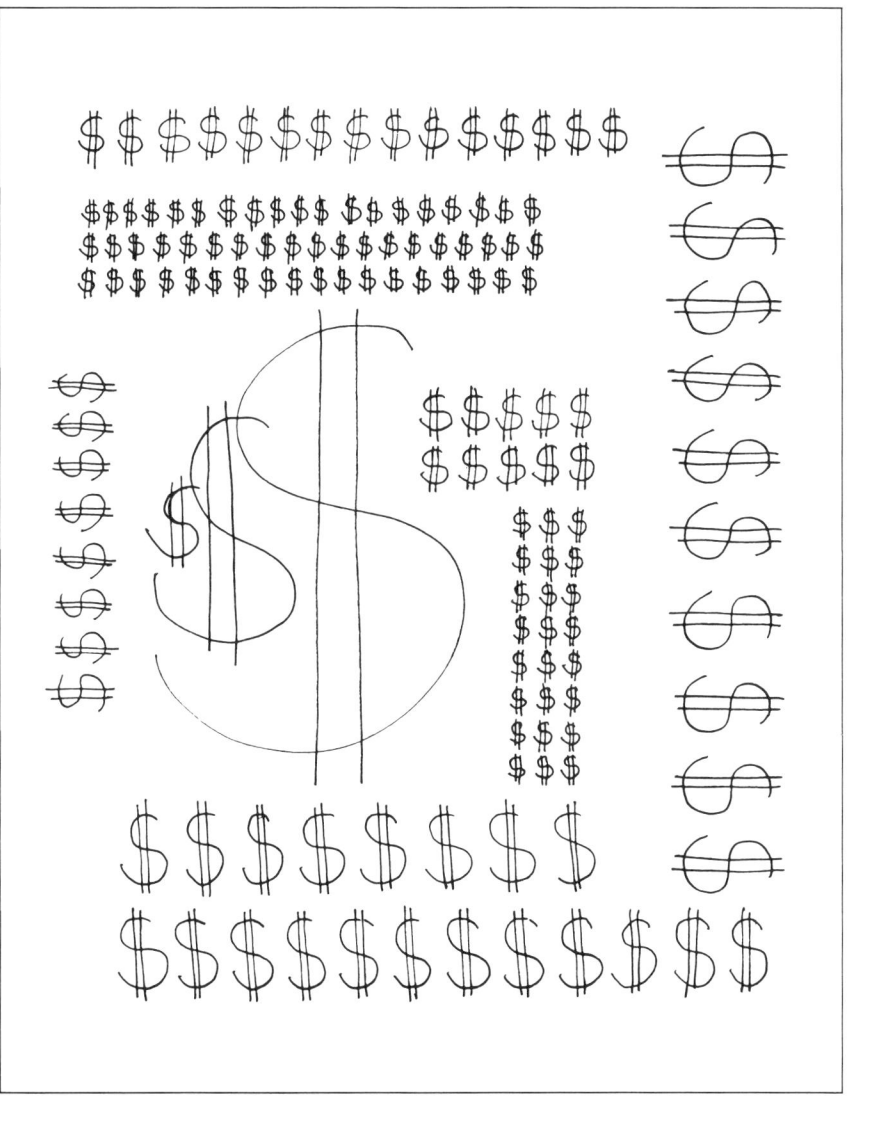

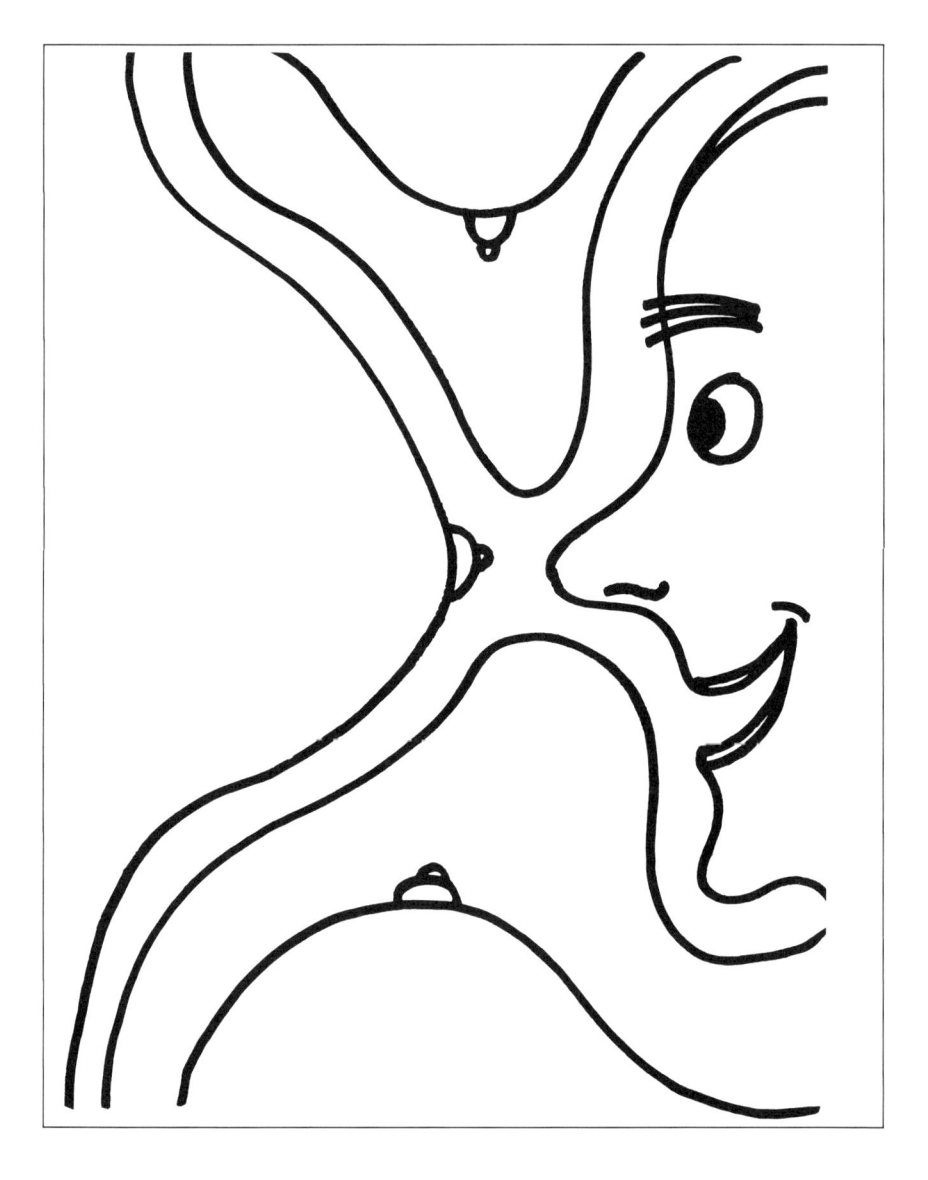

Notes taken by a management consultant during a presentation by his group on improving employees' note-taking techniques.

How to Answer a Question with a Question

If you don't know the answer to a question, come up with one of your own. Make sure your voice has the unmistakable Ring of Authority. Always go into details. The more technical your question, the better your chances to confuse.

Some questions you can always ask:

Who? Who invented the product? Who is using it? Who is not using it? Who is the competition?

What? What does he or she propose you should do with the information? What good does it do? What are the alternatives?

When? When did it happen?

Where? Where did the information come from? Where has it been used?

Why? Why is it so important? Why not take this up at the next meeting? Why ask now?

How? How would the information affect future plans? How much will it cost?

"A great idea!"

A good way to keep things going is to thank the participant for his or her contribution. Do not be stingy with praise. Giving credit where credit is due (or even when it is not) will: 1) help you in helping others to waste time, 2) show that you are the type who cares, 3) prove that you understand the problem, and— most important— 4) draw attention off the fact that it has been some time since *you* came up with an idea.

How to Add Confusion to Confusion

Sprinkle your conversation with acronyms. Rather than admit ignorance, your listeners will pretend they know exactly what the letters stand for. ***By being incomprehensible, you will be that much closer to taking command of the situation.***

DON'T SAY	SAY
Standard operating procedure	**SOP**
Administrative point of view	**APOV**
Management information system	**MIS**
Organizational development department	**ODD**
Return on investment	**ROI** (say Roy)
Organizational climate	**OC** (pronounced Ock)
Chief executive office	**CEO** (See-oh)
Management objectives	**MO** (Moe)
Small Business Administration	**SMABAD**
Area of dominant influence	**ADI** (Add-ee)
Wall Street Journal	**WASTREEJ**

Accountants, treasurers, and other financial types have a distinct advantage in using initial letters. In their discussions of corporate liabilities, for example, they can dip into the IRS's own long list of abbreviations specifically designed to confuse taxpayers. A quick sampling:

Adjusted Gross Income	**AGI**
Total Positive Income	**TPI**
Information Returns Programs	**IRP**
Coordinated Examination Program	**CEP**
Statistics of Income	**SOI**
Treasury Office of Tax Analysis	**TOTA**

Initials are especially useful if they have more than one interpretation, as, for example, AAA (Agricultural Adjustment Administration, Amateur Athletic Association, American Athletic Association, Automobile Association of America, Amateur Astronomers Association, a favorable credit rating, and the name of a New York City locksmith).

If possible, use abbreviations that are most likely to perplex your listeners. Toss them in casually as if you had used them for years and finally discovered what they stand for.

DON'T SAY	SAY	DON'T SAY	SAY
comprehensive	comp	executive	exec
subscriptions	subs	perquisite	perk
biography	bio	enclosure	enc
corporation	corp	maximum	max
magazine	mag	minimum	min
superimposition	super	introduction	intro
superintendent	super	preparation	prep
superior	super	schedule	sched
cumulative audience	cum	second	sec
picture	pix	signature	sig
promotion	prom	stenography	steno

In explaining your position, make use of trade jargon intelligible only to insiders, if even to them. Remember, computerese will not confound programmers. On the contrary, they just might understand better than you what you're talking about. Instead, use computerese when speaking to advertising people; advertisingese to programmers; legalese to marketing people; marketingese to lawyers, and so on.

> In my considered opinion, these are prepaid expenses, not deferred charges. As such they can certainly be classified as current assets.

> It has almost everything. CPU, RAM and ROM, I/O, electronics all on one card with the CPU housing. Not to mention the peripherals attachable to the boards.

> I'd rather go to the fifty top SMSA's and concentrate on indies. That may give us the best CPM's yet, even better than a whole bunch of 25+ network Nielsens.

The days of soft funding are over. Time has come to legitimize our goals, prioritize our communications objectives, and start interfacing with the budgetary.

That authority I would say comes under the exclusive substantive rule-making function of the FTC under section six of the act.

$$N - \frac{(R)\ (1-R)\ (C)^2}{E^2} \text{ Right?}$$

If you have just finished business school and have received your MBA (Master of Business Administration), you can speak authoritatively on any subject. Start your sentences with "today ..." as often as you can. This will put those in place who feel they are the leftovers from another generation, or almost everyone over twenty-five.

These Catchy Phrases Will Work Anytime and Anyplace

1. Look at it from a long range point of view...
2. In the last analysis...
3. In line with next year's projections...
4. In today's tight economy...
5. In the course of business
6. Nothing stays still
7. Money isn't everything
8. Let's look at the bottom line
9. What we need is capital
10. What we need is some fresh blood
11. What we need is an open mind
12. We're all on a fast track
13. Get our money's worth
14. You are the best
15. We don't want to support the IRS
16. Throwing good money after the bad
17. Between a rock and a hard place
18. You've got to spend money to make money
19. Now, if we can only keep our expenses under control...
20. The integrity of our management
21. The Year 2000 is not that far away...
22. Back then...
23. It's the good old American way
24. Ours is the free-enterprise system
25. Common sense suggests that...
26. You only get what you pay for
27. Our sleeves are rolled up

How to Change the Subject While You Still Can

Staying on a single topic for any length of time not only suggests a lack of imagination on your part, but runs the risk of bringing the meeting to an end and forcing attendees to return to their original offices.

Keeping the discussion on the same track lacks the surprise element.

As chairperson, it is your responsibility to keep the conversation going off in several directions all at the same time. The more you can branch off, the better your chances to draw out the meeting. Encourage participants to address each other directly, particularly if they are sitting at opposite ends of the table but still within shouting distance. This is known as Group Dynamics, and it allows *you* to lean back in your chair and let the meeting run itself.

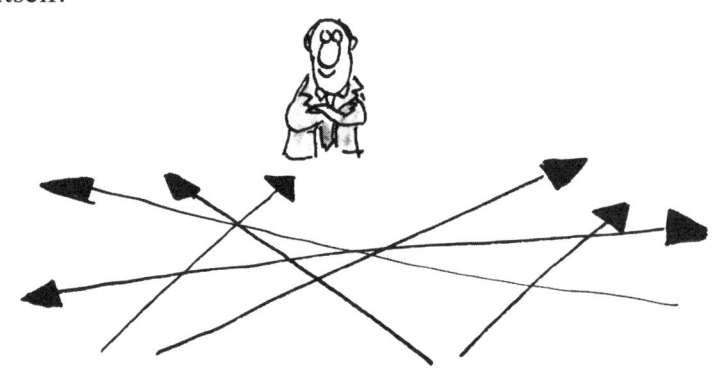

A Few (or Perhaps Not So Few) Words About Brainstorming

Meetings that are supposed to generate a free exchange of ideas—referred to as Brainstorming to suggest some kind of cerebral activity—have been a boon to people anxious to have meetings offering them a sense of accomplishment.

Brainstorming sessions have given birth to many ideas, some new and some not so new. When people get together and are encouraged to talk, they do shed their inhibitions. The following is a hypothetical example:

PETER (*excited*): Hey, I've got a great idea!

(*Everyone looks at Peter with anticipation.*)

DICK: You gonna tell us about it?

BOB (chairperson): Shhh! Let Peter tell us what he has in mind. That's what brainstorming is all about.

GROUP (*all together*): Hear! Hear!

PETER (*holding up a sketch of an egg*): Does anyone know what this is?

(*There is a long, thoughtful pause. Alice, a young woman, tentatively raises her hand.*)

ALICE: It's an egg. I recognize the shape because I always have two of them for breakfast.

PETER: Right! Now, here's my idea. We all know how easily round objects roll on the ground.

(*Group nods in unison, except for one man, Harold.*)

HAROLD: Yeah. And so what?

BOB: Harold, please. We're not here to make judgments. Let Peter go on with his proposal. [*He leans forward looking at Peter.*] Go ahead. We're here to listen.

PETER (*growing excited*): Suppose we attach three egg-shaped objects to the bottom of a vehicle. Wouldn't that make it move faster?

DOROTHY: Why not attach four?

PETER (*magnanimously*): Okay, four.

HAROLD: Wouldn't eggs make for a bumpy ride? Up and down. Up and down. I get nervous just thinking about it.

PETER (*glaring at Harold*): You have a better idea?

HAROLD: Yes [*holds up a quick pencil sketch of a circle*]. How about something like this?

ALICE: It looks like a doughnut to me. I know. I have one with my eggs every morning.

HAROLD (*making a face*): Eggs and doughnuts. Yuk!

BOB: No value judgments, please.

PETER (*looking at Harold's sketch, slightly taken aback*): Same thing, Harold. Only you've modified it somewhat.

HAROLD: Mine would run better.

SEVERAL VOICES: Do you have a name for your invention, Harold?

HAROLD: I call it the *wheel*.

CARL (*speaking up for the first time*): Hasn't the wheel been invented already?

BOB: Carl, let's not be negative.

CHAPTER SIX

Creating the right atmosphere

As CHAIRPERSON you must see to it that everyone feels comfortable, so he or she will come to the next meeting. A good turnout shows you are a popular figure, an effective leader. Poor turnout can be a problem. Nothing is more embarrassing than an empty conference room with you sitting at the head of the table all by yourself.

Basically, you will find that there are three types of meetings: 1) formal, 2) informal, and 3) very informal.

You can tell at a glance which is which by the way people sit on their chairs. At a formal meeting, members try their best to sit up straight. With most of the weight on the lower part of the human body, this pose can be as demanding as standing at attention. Not many people can hold it for an extended period of time. The record is 40 minutes and 26 seconds as of this writing— a remarkable feat by any standard. It was pulled off with aplomb by a striving, upwardly mobile young executive in top physical condition and who had several years of training in Hatha Yoga. Most people fall off their chairs much sooner than that.

Facial expressions at a formal meeting.

Formal meetings have proven to put such a strain on the participants both physically and emotionally that they are held only on special occasions, as for example, when taking an official photograph of the board of directors for next year's financial report. But even then, the posture is maintained for only a moment or two. After the picture has been taken, everybody heads for the nearest bar for a breather.

Devaney Stock Photos

If shoulders are sagging, heads are rolling back and forth, and legs are draped over, around and on top of the chairs, much in the manner of man's primatial ancestry, the ape, then you are probably looking at a *very* informal meeting.

Informal   *More informal*   *Excessively informal*

56

IN THEIR PRIVATE OFFICES, executives prefer to put their legs on their desks, as opposed to wrapping them around the chair. There are good reasons for this. Comfort is one; the weight is more evenly distributed this way, much like lying in bed. The position also causes the blood to flow in the general direction of the brain, which is supposed to generate some activity there.

The more years he has spent with the company, the more adept he becomes at stretching out his full anatomy behind the desk. His relaxed, devil-may-care posture signifies self-confidence, a mastery of Fate, and an impressive lack of concern over crises that would cause lesser men to fidget with papers on the desk top. By gazing at the ceiling in a near horizontal position he can hide his face; no one will see that he is fast asleep.

Many executives learn to cut down on wasted energy by moving the telephone across the desk with the inside sole of their feet. This saves them the effort from having to lean forward.

Unfortunately, the situation is not quite that simple around the conference table. Only the chairperson at the head has the room to stretch out comfortably.

All legs on the table would create a problem.

It is the chairperson's responsibility to prove that the meeting has a *purpose*—be that so or not. The company, after all, is paying not only for the people who go there but also for coffee and doughnuts.

It is for this reason that placed before every participant—even the chairperson—should be a yellow pad, preferably legal size. The sight of fresh pads at every seat seems purposeful indeed. It shows that the chairperson fully expects that something worth putting on paper will come up during discussion. Moreover, legal pads make excellent coasters on which to set a coffee cup. Some people even use them for napkins.

Management experts often want to know: Is it possible to conduct a business meeting without coffee? The answer is no, of course. Sipping coffee ranks high among activities at a meeting. It may yet be one of the highlights much as is dinnertime on a two-week cruise on the Atlantic Ocean. *In fact, having coffee and doughnuts at company expense is often considered as good a reason as any for holding a meeting in the first place.*

A cup of coffee gives everyone something with which to keep occupied. It can be held in the hands, stared at, put down, picked up again, raised to the mouth, sniffed, and even drunk.

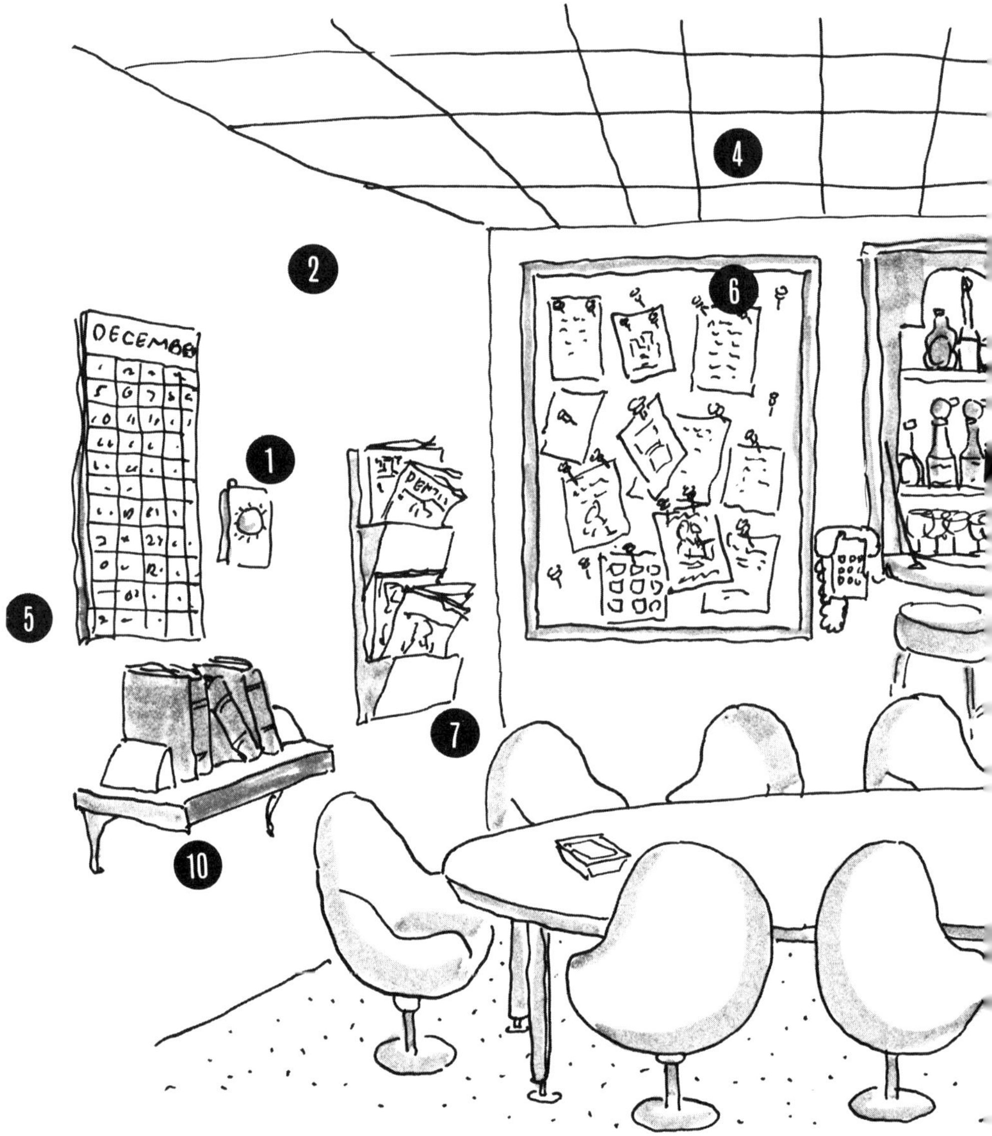
4
2
6
1
5
7
10

The Modern Conference Room

*Amenities abound. **1)** Thermostat adjusts temperature automatically as the hot air emanating from around the table causes it to rise. **2)** Wall is painted in subdued pastels to enable people to relax and catch up on lost sleep. **3)** Dimmer keeps light from glaring into people's eyes for the same reason. **4)** Acoustic ceiling tiles absorb loud noises that might keep someone awake. **5)** Calendar hanging on the wall emphasizes that time is money in business. It also shows what day it is for those who may be off three or four days. **6)** Corkboard holds sketches, charts, and other documentation that work is in progress. **7)** Rack holds publications containing comic strips, crossword puzzles, entertainment guides, lottery winners, daily racing forms, and the "Help Wanted" section of the newspaper. **8)** Built-in bar is for those who believe in breaks other than for coffee. **9)** Bolt on door prevents people from leaving. **10)** Bookshelf has something for those who like to curl up with a good book.*

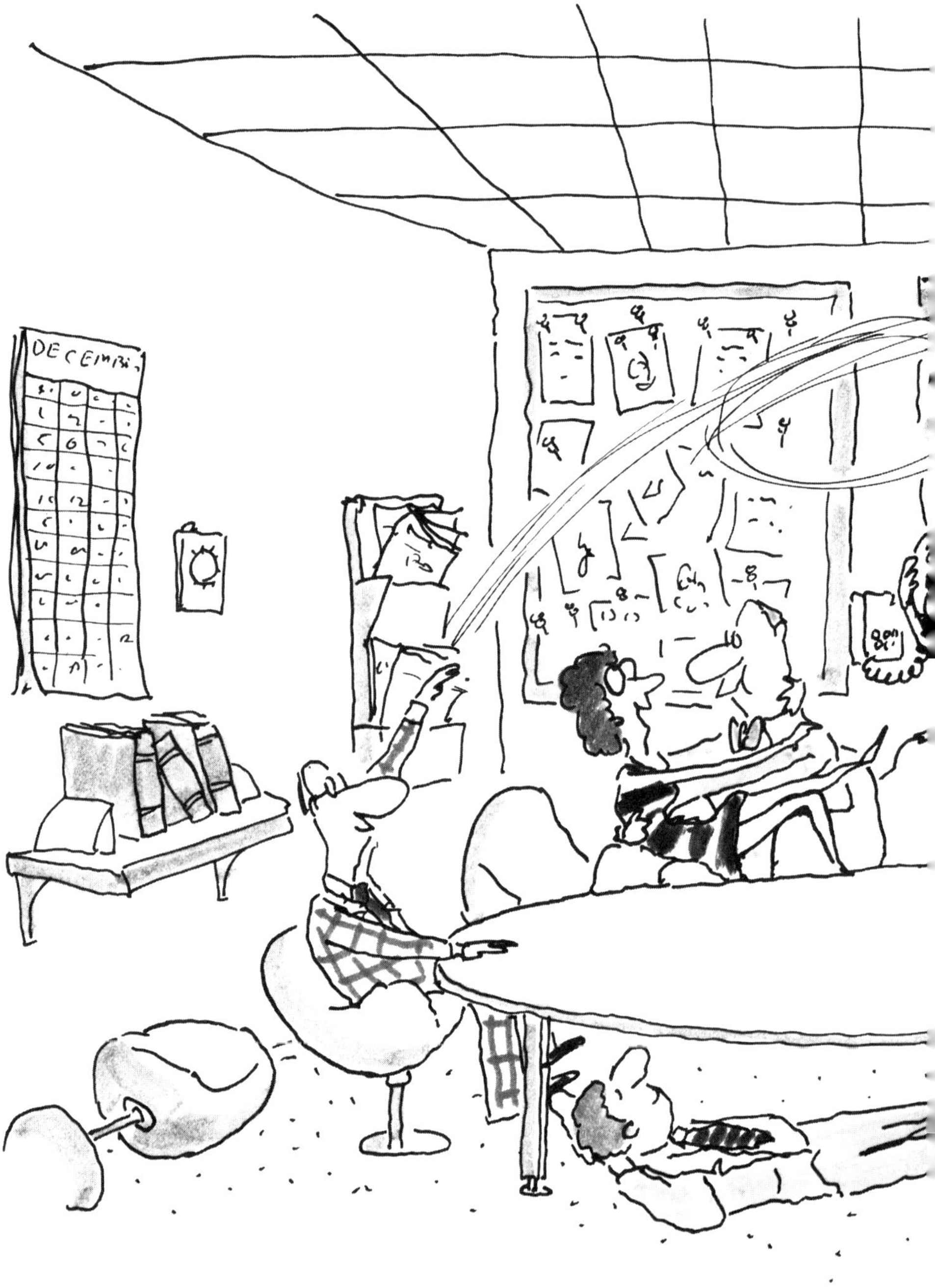

The trend these days is toward keeping meetings informal, uninhibited, and unencumbered by too many company rules.

CHAPTER SEVEN

How to act organized even if you're not

Interestingly enough, corporations like to refer to themselves as "organizations." *The word implies the presence of a System.* For those who need convincing, there are flow charts, organizational diagrams, financial graphs, and of course elaborately designed manuals on corporate policies, office procedures, interoffice communication, vacation schedules, sick leaves, employment insurance and pension programs, and the changing of typewriter ribbons. And there are manuals written to help explain manuals.

The System enables executives to follow rules established by the corporation and, when things go wrong, blame the results on the makers of the rules. Rules make it possible to appear well-organized at all times. To appear well-organized is the sign of a Skilled Administrator, a more important attribute than say, good judgment. Chairing a meeting offers a special opportunity for such a person to demonstrate his talent. *It takes careful planning and considerable administrative ability to be able to stretch planning a one hour meeting into an all-day conference.*

No meeting is complete without an agenda. It shows that you're not the type who leaves things to chance. For this reason, it is essential that the agenda appear well thought-out, thorough, and substantial, *even if it contains no information.* Two sheets are better than one; three sheets are better than two. An agenda more than four sheets shows you really made an effort, especially if the typing is neat, and the sheets are stapled together. Attach people's biographies, copy of last meeting's agenda, an article from *The New York Times,* if you can. An added advantage of a well-padded presentation is that no one will bother to go through it.

Triple-spaced lines will make the agenda look longer. Use even more space between paragraphs. At least half the area on the page should be taken up with margins on the sides, top and bottom. About a hundred words per page should be your average; more than that may cut down the number of pages and make the agenda appear skimpier.

As further proof of your scientific turn of mind, always group, sub-group, sub-sub-group, and sub-sub-sub-group all your material. Use caps and a new line for each category. Lines should be short and to the point, consisting of a word or two—never more than six. Use abbreviations. Remember you want to fill up your space not only horizontally but also *vertically.*

Alphabetize and/or number each item on the page. Use asterisks, double asterisks, triple asterisks, and sprinkle your texts with scholarly terms such as "to wit". Summarize the purpose of the meeting. Then summarize your summary on a separate sheet.

ALL WELL-ORGANIZED SPEAKERS use charts to make their points, even if they don't have any. Charts serve three purposes. They

- suggest an orderly approach
- save the speaker from having to say much
- give the speaker something to do.

All charts should be prepared with these purposes in mind. The following hints may help you to achieve the effect you want.

No chart is complete without arrows. They give the viewer a sense of direction.

Lines suggest that one thing leads to another— a reassuring thought.

Bars and divided circles attest to the speaker's systematic approach.

Letters and numbers, particularly alongside vertical and horizontal lines, lend credibility to the presentation.

For clarification, use a pointer.

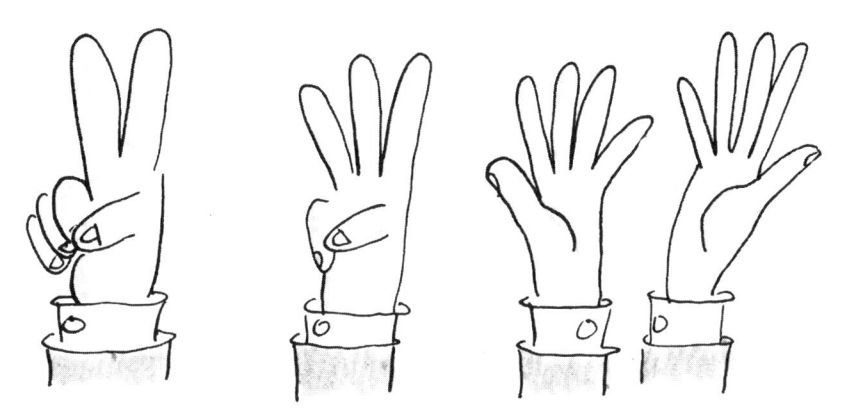

Fingers show order of succession. Remember: *Yours is a logical mind.*

The Problem.

Is There a Problem?

Everyone Says There Is a Problem.

So Let's Proceed Accordingly.

Flip charts emphasize the highlights of your talk.

How to Use Statistics to Prove Anything

Nothing is as persuasive as a long column of facts and figures, a compilation so complex as to be impossible to follow. No one is about to take issue with facts especially when they are backed up by computations, equations, extrapolations, interpolations, permutations, extraction of roots, harmonical progressions, quotients, alternations, and other forms of higher mathematics the people in your audience feel they should understand when they do not. If you are as confused by your presentation as your audience, no matter. Throw in more numbers, more statistical data. Note the following dialogue:

BOB (vice-president of sales of a cat food company): As the sales manager for the southeastern territory, how do you explain our poor showing in that area?

JOHN (sales manager for southeastern territory): Based on data just received from the Bureau of Economic Analysis, per capita income rose a mere 12 percent last year. With inflation being what it is, this has meant less than a 1.4-percent increase in real income, cat owners included. In truth, we're ahead of the game.

BOB (after a long pause trying to absorb the information): I'm afraid I don't follow you, John.

JOHN: Okay, let me put that information into plain English. As you know, spending has dropped 3.4 times faster nationwide than general purchasing power. This means that our average customer today has a full 2.5 percent less to spend on our product than a year ago.

BOB: But we're selling cat food ... cats have to eat just the same.

JOHN: I have no idea what cats do, Bob. I don't know what they think. I'm not a feline psychologist. All I know is what the figures tell me. There are 35 million cat owners in the United States, according to Pet Supplies Marketing. This is a 110-percent increase in the last ten years. Eighty-eight percent buy cat food for their pets every three weeks, spending over $900 million a year, the equivalent of $11.50 for each person in the country. So says National Analysts. Now our share today is 16 percent. Isn't that so?

BOB (bewildered): Yes.

JOHN: Well, there you are. The numbers tell the whole story. Twenty-nine percent of that goes on dry, 59 percent on canned, and 12 percent on moist cat food. Isn't that so?

BOB: Yes, but I'm still puzzled. . . .

JOHN: Two and two makes four. That's all there is to it, Bob.

BOB (giving up): Of course.

Always cite sources of reference. The longer the title, the more impressive. ***Throw in names, dates, places. List one after another, rattling them off so fast no one will be able to follow you.***

Don't be afraid to use statistics that have nothing to do with the subject at hand. Your audience will appreciate your Awareness, Respect for Facts, and Photographic Memory.

> Rabbits live six years.

> Only two nationalities— the Russians and the Poles—outdrink Americans.

> Clergymen rate highest in prestige.

> Every toilet flush disposes of six to eight gallons of water.

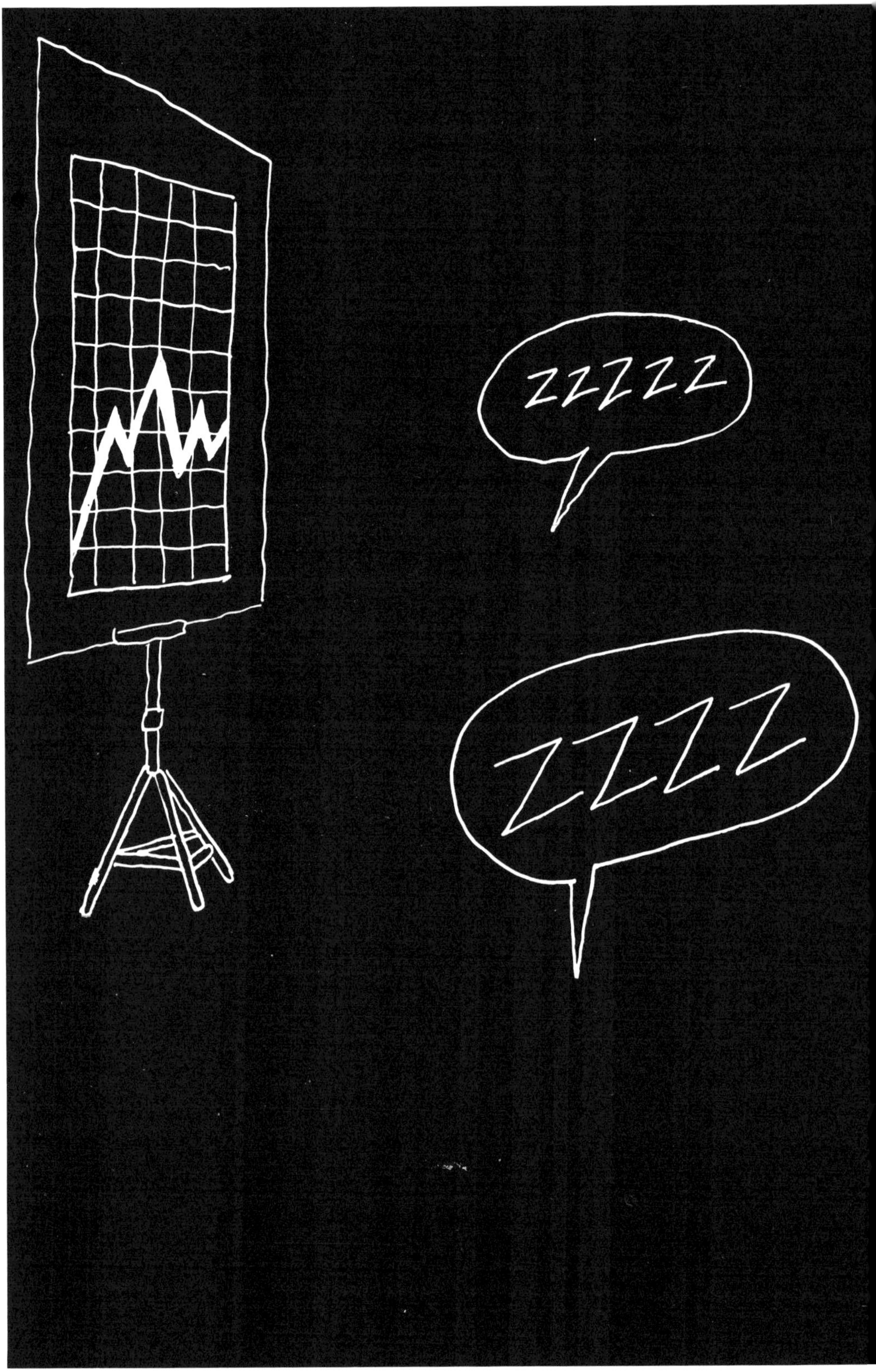
ZZZZZ
ZZZZ

Particularly useful are slide presentations. With the lights turned off, they allow the audience to engage in their favorite pastime.

CHAPTER EIGHT

What every chairperson should know about problem people around the conference table

T HE NUMBER of Problem People at a meeting rises in direct proportion to the size of the gathering. Say you have twenty-five attendees. That means you have twenty-five Problem People, a conservative estimate.

As a chairperson, it is your responsibility to deal with troublemakers. This may not be as easy as it sounds. You cannot send somebody to the principal's office for bad behavior. You cannot make them stay in the conference room after the meeting. The ways of a corporation are different from that.

Fortunately there are long-established traditions which you can follow. For example, office etiquette suggests at no time should there be more than ten people talking simultaneously across the table at a meeting particularly when the chairperson is talking too. Also, no one must shout, scream, howl, or bellow— at least not until all other modes of communicating have already been exhausted.

Most corporations urge employees to use their fists only as a last resort in settling differences of opinions. Should it come to blows, most companies know their reputation is at stake. *So they insist on a clean fight.* This means that as the person in charge you must see to it that there is no kicking, hitting below the belt, or rabbit punching. The fighter knocked out must take a count of ten, even if he is able to stand up. If he is hopelessly outclassed, you may try to stop the fight. Or alert an ambulance.

How to Keep Your Problem People Under Control (More or Less)

The Speechmaker: Took correspondence course in Effective Public Speaking and/or read Dorothy Sarnoff's *Speech Can Change Your Life*. Doesn't say much and takes his time saying it.

How to cope: Let him say his piece. The longer his speech, the longer the meeting will be.

The Yawner: Yawns often and loud. This wakes up the others.

How to cope: Yawning can be contagious. Try not to show yours.

The Bottom Liner: Lost without his or her calculator, this person has the answers printed out on tape and likes to read them out loud.

How to cope: Thank him or her for the information, ignore it, and move quickly to the next item on the agenda.

The Devil's Advocate: Knows why using someone else's idea could cost you your job.

How to cope: Accept his point of view. He's probably right.

The Early Leaver: Walks out of the room before the meeting ends.

How to cope: Don't be jealous.

The Late-Comer: Shows up long after the meeting begins.

How to cope: Tell that person in great detail what has transpired before his arrival. That, too, will help make the meeting last longer.

CHAPTER NINE

How to keep from making a decision

As a CHAIRPERSON you may be called upon to make a decision on occasion. Accept this with good grace, try not to get flustered. It goes with the job.

Your ability to postpone or, better yet, avoid making a decision altogether, will be a determining factor in your success with the company. Top-level executives, often referred to by themselves and others as Decision Makers, usually decide early in their careers never to be caught in the decision-making process. That is one of the first decisions they make and, if everything works out as planned, their last.

Most decisions are made toward the conclusion of a meeting when everyone wants to go home. This is when you have to be most careful not to fall into the trap set for unwary chairpersons. One way to protect yourself is to offer a Brief Summation of the meeting, known in corporate circles as the Review, Recap, Rehash, Sum and Substance, or Just a Few Words. The most effective Brief Summations are those that are given in a steady monotonous voice and last about twice as long as the meeting that preceded them.

Brief summations make it possible to avoid having to:

- Come up with anything new
- Pass judgment on any of the recommendations made
- Make a decision

If asked at the end of your summation to comment on the meeting, tell your audience you most certainly are prepared to do so, but you wish to Hold Your Judgment in Abeyance.

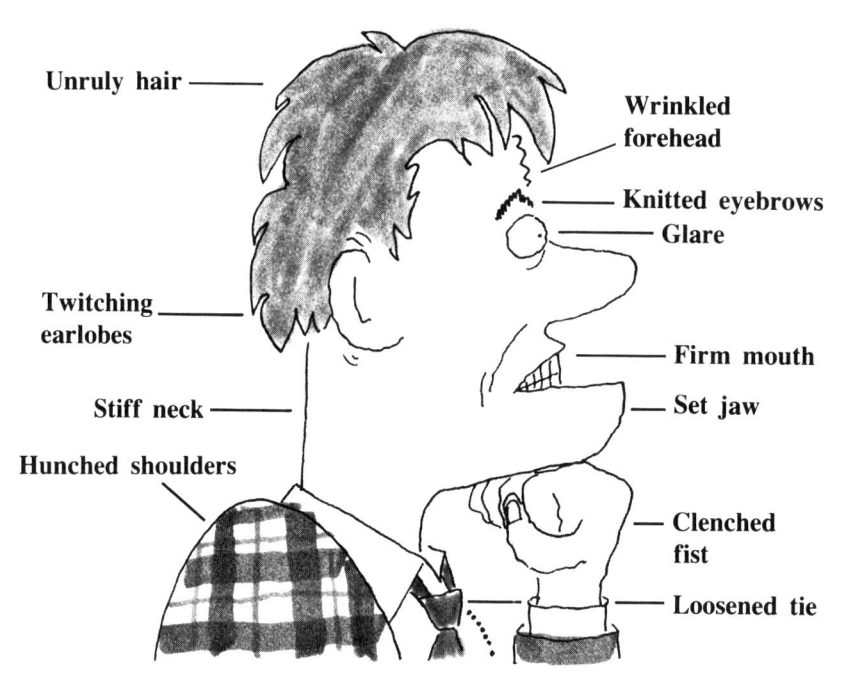

More important than making decisions is that you look like a Decision Maker.

INDECISIVE   DECISIVE

Learn how to rearrange your features for maximum effect.

Let the Lawyers Decide

Good executives insist on getting second, third, and fourth opinions on important matters. Some elicit as many as ten opinions to make sure everyone gets confused. *Getting more than one opinion not only indicates sound business judgment, but makes it possible to postpone decision making indefinitely, or at least until no one remembers what it was that had to be decided in the first place.*

A good move is to send proposals—here you must always refer to them as "papers"—to the Legal Department for final approval. *Lawyers welcome papers; reading them helps to while the time away.* The more lawyers put on your case, the more popular you will be with the department. What's more, the better the chances that you will never see the proposal again or that it will emerge so changed that any resemblance to the original will be purely coincidental.

It behooves counsel to spend Adequate Time on studying the papers submitted to His Office. A few weeks, a few months, or a few years will usually do it.

Send It Out for Research

All projects can use More Research. Your image as an executive will be enhanced considerably when you ask for additional information on which to base Sound Decisions.

Having made the decision to send the proposal out for further research, you can sit back and relax. Progress comes to a halt till the Boys (or Girls) in the Research Department Have Done Their Homework.

There is no end to the number of questions you can ask your Research Department to investigate. It really doesn't matter whether you already know the answer or it can be found in the Yellow Pages. Asking several thousands of people the same question is far more impressive and certainly more time-consuming. All said and done, you can then proceed to Reduce Your Findings to Writing. Particularly important is a computerized analysis at the end of the report. This should help you tabulate the facts that may have been obvious to everyone for some time but which have never been revealed in so orderly a fashion.

Try going the full circle. This will make it possible for you to end up exactly where you started many months before. The procedure is not as complicated as it may seem at first. A case in point is a recommendation made by an Art Department of a food company about the color of its new canned goods. Not to be rushed, the executive in charge of the project decided (note the word "decided") to set off his artists' suggestion (azure blue) against other possible colors. "There is a whole color spectrum out there," he reminded them and everyone agreed that this was indeed the case. He called on the Research Department for help. That move was applauded as an example of prudent decision making. Step by step, here is what took place:

| Azure blue | **VS.** | Cobalt green |

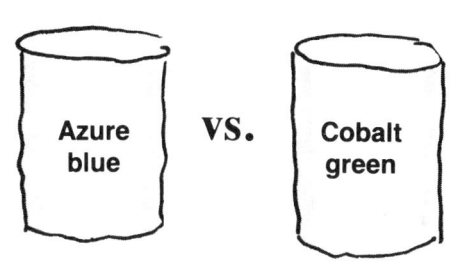

Cobalt green won. So he proceeded with the test ...

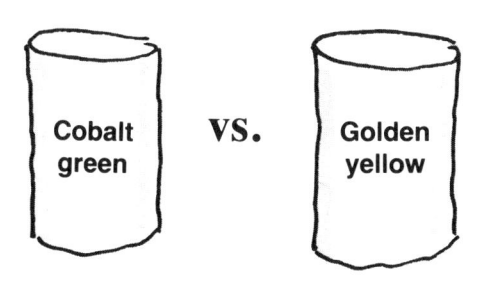

| Cobalt green | **VS.** | Golden yellow |

Golden yellow won.

| Golden yellow | **VS.** | Burnt orange |

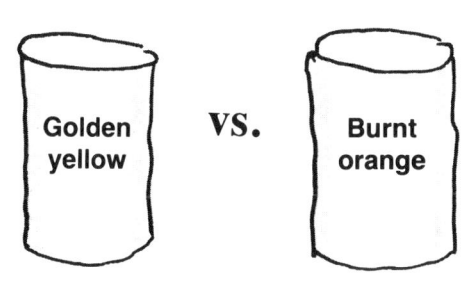

Golden yellow won again.

Still not completely satisfied, he had the Research Department mail six-page, meticulously worded questionnaires to 2,000 carefully selected homes in the middle to high-middle income areas of four typical mid-American cities, conduct flash card street interviews in various high-traffic intersections, and take the problem to several focus groups for in-depth discussions. He also called a thousand people between the hours of 5 and 6 P.M. to find out about their color preferences. Moreover, he polled his wife, mother-in-law, and two children—six and four years of age. Finally, he superimposed on the data various variables, such as Rate of Employment, Gross National Product, and Long Range Weather Forecast. Based on the information, he then instructed the Research Department to proceed <u>at once</u> with their Analysis since time was running short.

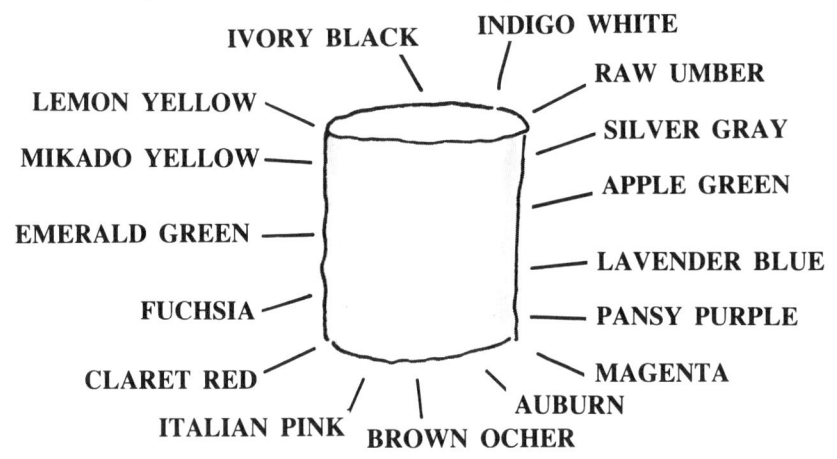

```
                 IVORY BLACK   INDIGO WHITE
                         \      /  RAW UMBER
       LEMON YELLOW  \    |   /  /
                      \   |  /  /   SILVER GRAY
       MIKADO YELLOW —    |     —
                          |         APPLE GREEN
       EMERALD GREEN —    |     — LAVENDER BLUE
                          |
            FUCHSIA  /    |     — PANSY PURPLE
                    /     |      \  MAGENTA
         CLARET RED    /  |  \   AUBURN
            ITALIAN PINK  BROWN OCHER
```

Brown ocher emerged as the clear winner. To make absolutely sure he was on the right track, he tested brown ocher against azure blue, the color originally recommended by his Art Department.

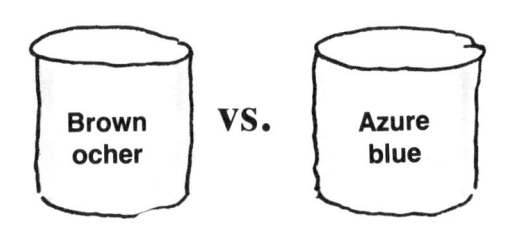

| Brown ocher | VS. | Azure blue |

Nine out of ten people favored azure blue over brown ocher. The executive was now in the position to announce the Results Supported by Research. He suggested his company go ahead with azure blue.

Should your research project be criticized as being too costly, recommend another research project. This one to find out how costs could have been cut.

IN THESE DAYS, high-tech yet may prove to be an executive's best friend. He or she can now pass on great amounts of information to data processing specialists who in turn feed it into computers which in turn will return the same but in a different form.

There is no program that cannot be expanded or modified so as to offer still another point of view on the same subject. As a decision maker you have the right to ask for additional information, if for no other reason but to find out if you were right the first time around. Up-to-date executives make it their business to store miles of printouts in their offices on shelves, desk tops, windowsills, or other places of high visibility whether or not they ever read the stuff.

ONE OF THE MOST EFFECTIVE WAYS to stop a recommendation from going any further is to ask for a Budget. Asking for a breakdown is a sure way to put your audience on the defensive, with you on the offensive.

It takes time and effort to prepare a budget, and there is a good chance that none will pass your muster if you don't want it to. Always, you can ask for a Revised Budget. That should keep you and several others busy for some time.

In postponing your final decision you can point to a new budget as being

- too high or
- too low.

You may cut or raise the proposed estimate any amount, that being one of the prerogatives of a decision maker. Or you can simply shelve the budget proposal for the time being. Inflation will render the figures obsolete and *thus, you will have still another chance to go through the decision-making process, and you will be able to cancel the entire project due to rising costs.*

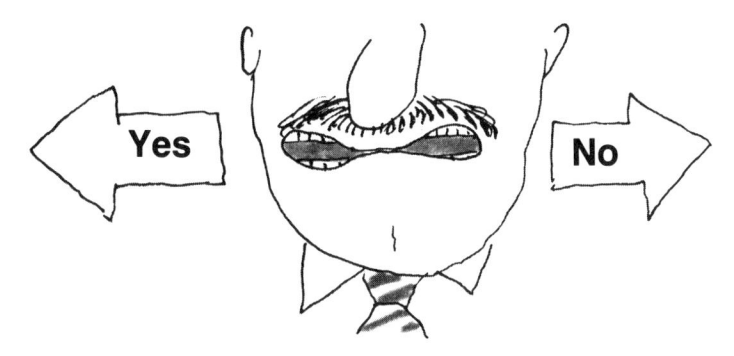

Your mouth has two sides. Use them both simultaneously.

Even when racing against a deadline, there is no reason to panic. ***Just make sure you don't lose your head and start offering specific solutions to specific problems.*** It is at such times you should be ready to bring up a Wide Variety of Alternatives. Remember that to choose between two solutions takes more time than having a single choice, perhaps more than twice as long. Three, four, or five alternatives are even more bewildering. Proponents will have to go back to the drawing board and start all over again.

Avoid committing yourself at all costs. Say that you are not the dictatorial type. All good executives have mastered the art of hemming and hawing. These phrases may start you on the right track:

On one hand . . . on the other hand	**And all that sort of thing**
So to speak	**And so it goes**
Under certain conditions	**Given the option**
Sort of	**Principally**
Kind of	**For the most part**
To a degree	**Whenever**
Everything being equal	**Whatever**
By and large	**Whichever**
In the long run	**Neither here nor there**
Generally speaking	**Here today, gone tomorrow**
All things considered	**Seems like**
To all intents and purposes	**On the other side of the coin**
As it were	**On the face of it**

At first glance
At a quick glance
Off the record
One way or another
As things go
God willing
In due time
By way of parenthesis
Depending on your point of view
Providing that
On the supposition that
If it so turns out
Unless
With a string to it
I'll venture to say
As like it or not
Presumably
There are a number of ways
You never can tell
In these uncertain times

In this volatile economy
The way things stand
But from a realistic point of view
On a good day
On a bad day
In broad terms
In words to that effect
Knock on wood (accompanied by your knocking on wood or your head)
In broad strokes
We could say
You could say
I could say
In a way
Depending on
Things change
Time marches on
There's always tomorrow
At this particular time

Be wary of numbers. Qualify your statement with:

Something like
Approximately
A ballpark figure
On the average
According to some sources
Based on current information
Polltakers may disagree but
In round numbers
Just a wild guess, of course
Depending on whom you talk to
Give and take a few million

About
Some say more
Some say less
Hard data not being available
At latest count
A well-kept secret
Washington says
Roughly
Not exactly but close enough
Unofficially

Keep them guessing:

I want to keep an open mind on this

Of course, you may have other ideas

I'm no expert on the subject

I realize that there are two sides to every question

Now let's take a vote on this

Food for thought

Something to stew over

Just throwing it on the table

That's one way to put it

You may or may not agree

For additional information on decisions you know you will never make, appoint a Task Force. Or two. Or three. Suggest that they get together often, which they will readily do. Task forces are also fond of holding Emergency Meetings. (An Emergency Meeting is any meeting called into session on short notice to find out whether there is in fact an emergency.) Finally, ask each Task Force to Make a Recommendation. *Chances are their proposals will be at cross purposes. This will enable you to form a new group to reconcile points of view.*

Committees established for the purpose of suggesting the formation of more committees are especially useful, almost as much as committees formed to check over the work of other committees.

Always appear to look for a consensus. It is at this point you should throw in your alternate suggestions. This will inspire people in the group to come up with a few of their own suggestions and then fight among themselves as to the merit of each. After an hour or so, say, "Looks like we have a hung jury." Smiling, set a date for another meeting.

There comes a time when you will have to close the meeting—as, for example, at the end of the day. Build up to it. Glance at your watch every minute or so. This will remind your audience of the passing of time. Wind your watch, hold it to your ear to see if it's running even though you know it is, and shake it well. Then, ask someone else what time it is. Mumble something about how time passes, you wish there were more hours in the day, life is short, etc. Sooner or later, your audience will get the message.

Always end the meeting on a Positive Note. Any of these phrases will do:

"This has been an excellent meeting."

"I can't tell you how much I appreciate your contributions. Thank you for bearing with me. It's been a most productive session."

"We're all richer for the experience."

"Everything we set out to accomplish today has been accomplished."

"You were just great."

"Mission accomplished."

Having said that, you may now set a time for getting together the next morning to continue the discussion.

Never close a meeting with the words, "Let's sleep on it." Your audience just may take you up on it.

CHAPTER TEN

How to meet for business outside the office and accomplish absolutely nothing

HAVING MEETINGS OUTSIDE the office offers a number of advantages, all of which warrant serious consideration.

In a restaurant, you can have food and drinks, though not necessarily in that order, to help mix business with pleasure. ***In regard to drinking, it bears mentioning that the much-criticized, "three-martini lunches" appear to be on their way out.***

Another important step concerning three-martini lunches was the switch from martinis to Manhattans.

Among the benefits of talking business over lunch is the informality of it all. With no written agenda on the table, it is easier to skip from one subject to another. For example, you can summon the waiter—any time you want to talk to him at length and about any items on the menu. All waiters have an opinion about the food they serve, whether they had a chance tasting it. Moreover, you can always recommend dishes to others at the table. They will welcome the opportunity to talk about something so much more interesting than business.

Should the conversation drag, you can always order another round of drinks. There is much to be said for the fact that liquor breaks down inhibitions. That is why so many executives enjoy a snort now and then. Few could be classified as alcoholics. They simply go on a binge to enjoy each other's company, to drink to the health of the company who pays for it all, or to entertain a client who came to town mainly to have a good time. By definition, this puts them into the category of the "social drinker," and nothing more.

The Executive Sobriety Test at a Restaurant

1 DRINK	No effect except thirst for another.
2 DRINKS	State of euphoria. Confidence in the future of the corporation.
3 DRINKS	Shakes with laughter. Slaps people on the back.
4 DRINKS	Makes faces at the people at the next table.
5 DRINKS	Arrives at the conclusion that this is as good a time as any to set long-range corporate policy. Scribbles projected profits for the coming year on the tablecloth in indelible ink.
6 DRINKS	Hurries to the bathroom. Offers a toast to everyone in the restaurant upon returning. Buys drinks for those at the next table on the expense account. Sings "God Bless America" and takes a bow.
7 DRINKS	Walks an imaginary chalk line on the floor to prove his sobriety. Bumps into his chair and stumbles. He is escorted out the door by his partners who hail a taxi to take him home. Cabbie wants to be paid in advance.

How to Look Like Somebody in a Restaurant Without Being Anybody

Make sure the maître d' calls you by name.

Make sure the coat attendant calls you by name.

Make sure the bartender calls you by name.

Make sure the waiter calls you by name.

Make sure the wine steward calls you by name.

Make sure the busboy calls you by name.

IMPORTANT: Never order anything in English if the restaurant offers foreign cuisine.

DON'T SAY	SAY (ITALIAN)	SAY (SPANISH)	SAY (GREEK)
Bread	Pane	Pan	Psomi
Bottle	Bottiglia	Botella	Botilia
Water	Acqua	Aqua	Neró
Salt	Sale	Sal	Aláti
Sugar	Zucchero	Azúcar	Zákhari
Knife	Coltello	Cuchillo	Makhairi
Fork	Forchetta	Tenedor	Pirouni
Spoon	Cucchiaio	Cuchara	Koutáli
Waiter	Camarero	Camarero	Servitóros
Toilet	Gabinetto	Retrete	Méros

SAY (FRENCH)	SAY (JAPANESE)	SAY (YIDDISH)	SAY (ARABIC)
Pain	Pan	Broit	'Eish
Bouteille	Bin	Flasch	Azâza
Eau	Mizu	Vasser	Maiyeh
Sel	Shio	Salts	Malh
Sucre	Satoo	Tsukker	Sukkar
Couteau	Naifu	Messer	Sikkîneh
Fourchette	Fooku	Gopel	Shôka
Cuiller	Saji	Leffel	Malaka
Garçon	Kyuujinin	Kelner	Sufrâgi
Cabinet	Benjo	Abord	Kanîf

If you ask for wine, ask for it with style. Read the label and frown. Sniff the bouquet in the glass and look as if you're gathering important information.

Forehead furrowed

Eyes closed

Nose flared

Little finger extended

Close your eyes as you savor the wine. Never describe the wine simply as being "okay." Say "spicy," "delicate," "tart," "nutty," "brisk," "keen," "pungent," or "jejune" instead. As you open your eyes, exchange knowing glances with the person serving the drink and standing in attention waiting for your decision. Then glance at the label, comment on the vintage ("It was a good year"), break into a slow smile, and, after a long suspenseful silence, nod your approval.

In ordering a drink, make sure you specify the brand. "Wild Turkey" beats bourbon, "Chivas Regal" sounds better than scotch. Ignore the house brand altogether.

Never say "water." Ask for Perrier.

REMEMBER: Always complain about at least one dish on the menu. Loud enough so everyone can hear you.

As a host it behooves you to show that you intend to pay for the lunch. But make sure others get to the check before you do.

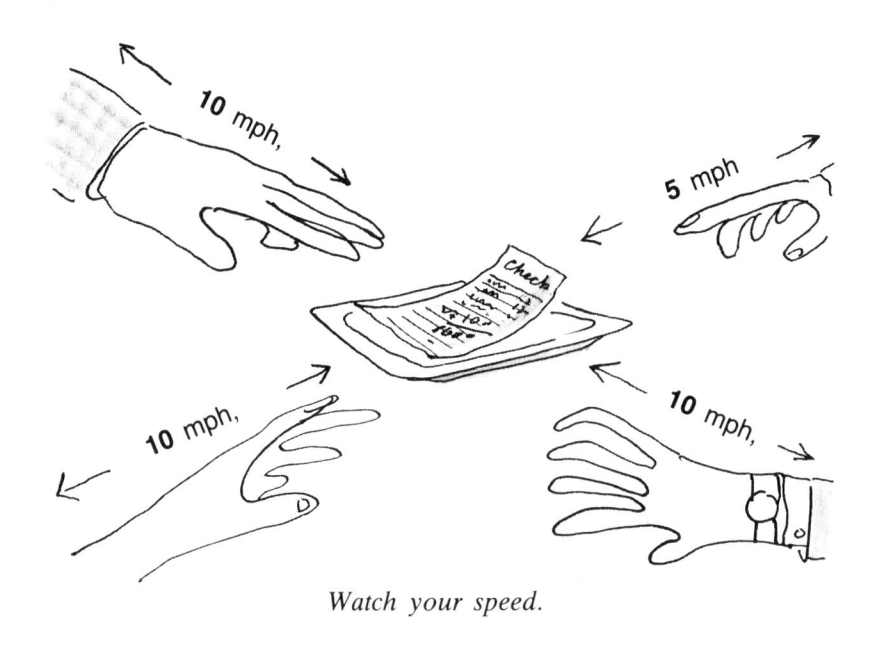

Watch your speed.

Smile and talk about the next lunchtime.

Next time, it's on me.

Conventions: How to Get the Least Out of the Most People

The purpose of a convention is to do business. There are two very good reasons for taking this approach. One is to let your spouse at home know that you're working hard. The other is to let the IRS know that the bill for your all-night stand at the bar, the cost of lost balls on the golf course, and your misguided bets at the crap table all were incurred while conducting business.

Much attention is being paid to the theme of the meeting, as moot as it may seem. This is the time companies recite their past achievements in the last fifty to a hundred years; the longer the history, the better. The occasion also lends itself to various forms of divination—a Glimpse into the Future, Crystal-gazing, a Look Ahead. Yesterday and Tomorrow both get ample coverage. Less is said about Today.

At first there might be some unrest among the attendees as they exchange notes among themselves or react to what is being said. Soon, however, as one speaker follows the next on the podium, the noise subsides as members of the audience quietly go to sleep... proving once again that this is a Business Meeting, not just a social gathering. In addition to speakers, there are many comely hostesses acting much like usherettes in a Broadway theater. These women are there to smile at all comers and pass out name tags to identify guests to strangers and guests to themselves in case they are too drunk to remember their own names.

For further proof that this is a business meeting, looseleaf binders are issued with logos permanently embossed on the cover. These are usually hardcover so they cannot be folded or crumpled into the shape of a ball in order to throw them in a wastepaper basket. Inside there is important information about the company and its purpose for having a convention so soon after the last one.

Recommended sites for business conventions with Hard Work as the keynote: Acapulco, Bahamas, Caribbean, Hawaii, Monte Carlo, Palm Beach, Rio de Janeiro, St. Moritz, St. Tropez, San Francisco, and São Paulo.

Below is a view of a hotel especially designed for holding business conventions: **1)** *Sun* **2)** *Excellent view* **3)** *19th hole* **4)** *Outdoor pool* **5)** *Tennis courts* **6)** *Grand Ballroom, theaters, full-size bars and restaurants* **7)** *Gambling casino*

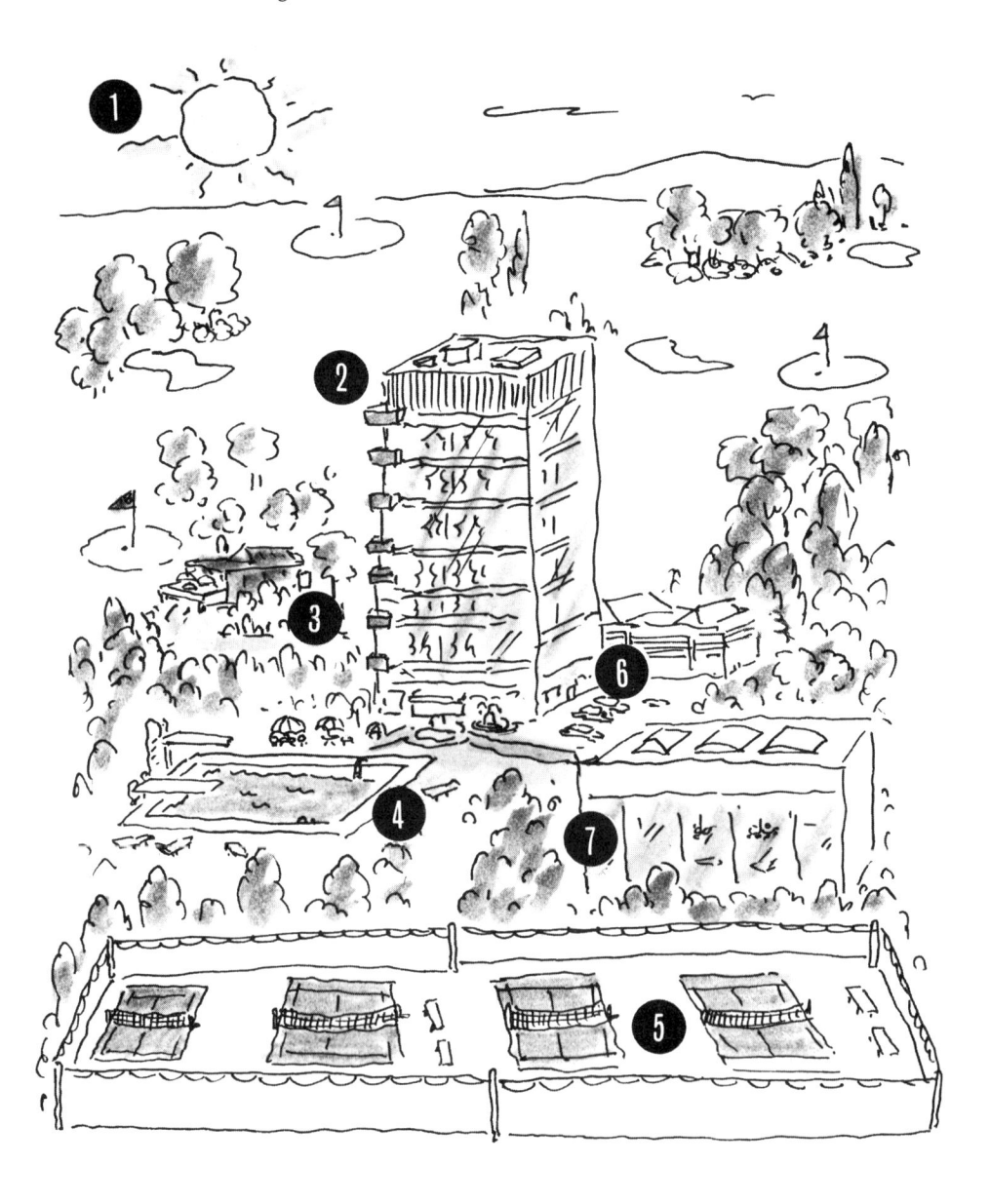

How to Organize a Large Meeting

Here is a one-day schedule for what is usually referred to as a "workshop." Note the early start. This is to emphasize that attendees mean business. If no one shows up, breakfast is carted back to the kitchen for the staff to enjoy what they had prepared.

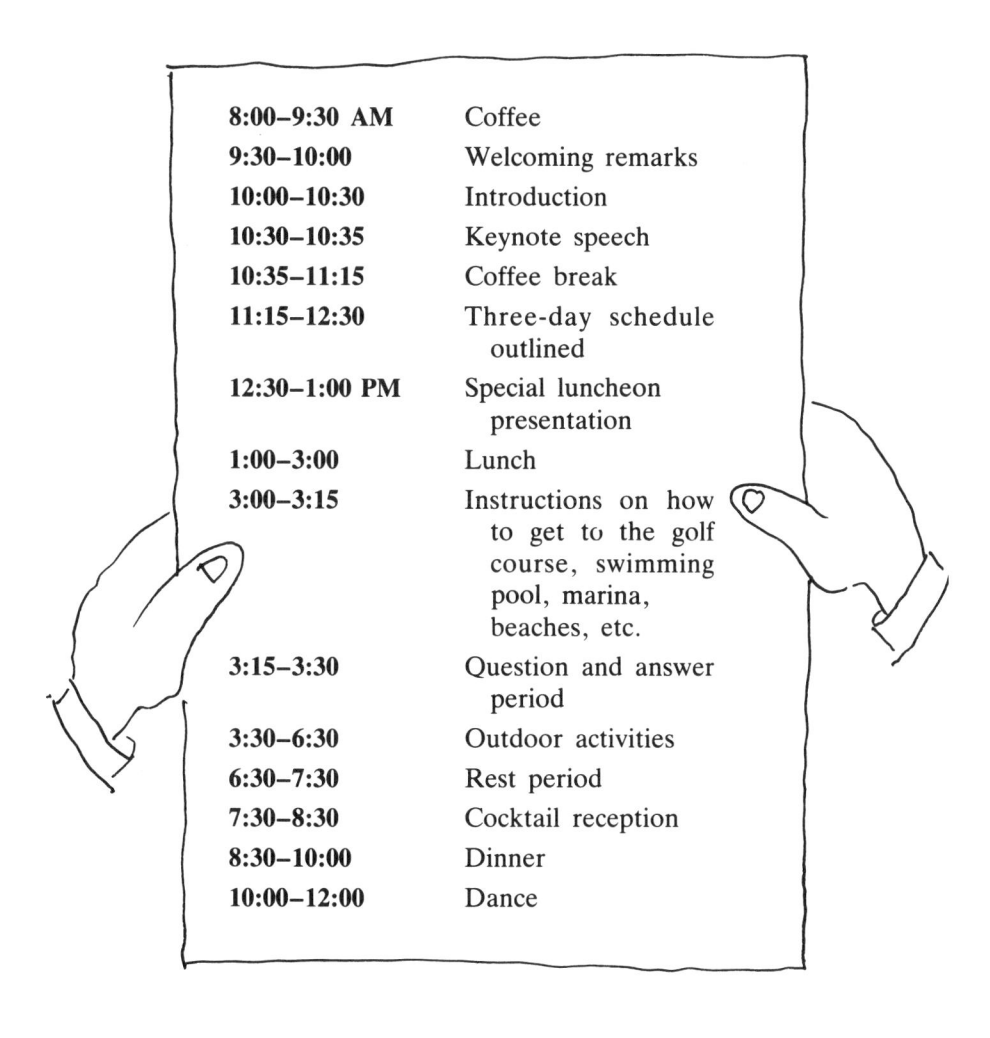

8:00–9:30 AM	Coffee
9:30–10:00	Welcoming remarks
10:00–10:30	Introduction
10:30–10:35	Keynote speech
10:35–11:15	Coffee break
11:15–12:30	Three-day schedule outlined
12:30–1:00 PM	Special luncheon presentation
1:00–3:00	Lunch
3:00–3:15	Instructions on how to get to the golf course, swimming pool, marina, beaches, etc.
3:15–3:30	Question and answer period
3:30–6:30	Outdoor activities
6:30–7:30	Rest period
7:30–8:30	Cocktail reception
8:30–10:00	Dinner
10:00–12:00	Dance

Seasoned speakers know how to make an impression on their audience without saying very much. 1) Banner sets the tone. 2) Microphone amplifies the voice to keep the audience awake. 3) Platform makes the speaker appear taller. 4) Alcoholic beverage enables speaker to relax. 5) Papers lend authority to the presentation even if they are blank. 6) News photographer, ostensibly representing the local press, keeps clicking his camera as if taking pictures of a celebrity and 7) among the people sitting at the table next to the speaker's stand is the person to introduce the person who is going to introduce the speaker.

A lot of preparation goes into making a presentation. Books can be very helpful.

Use live entertainment for change of pace.

THE BIGGEST YEAR EVER

WE SHAL[L]

GREAT!

FANTASTIC!

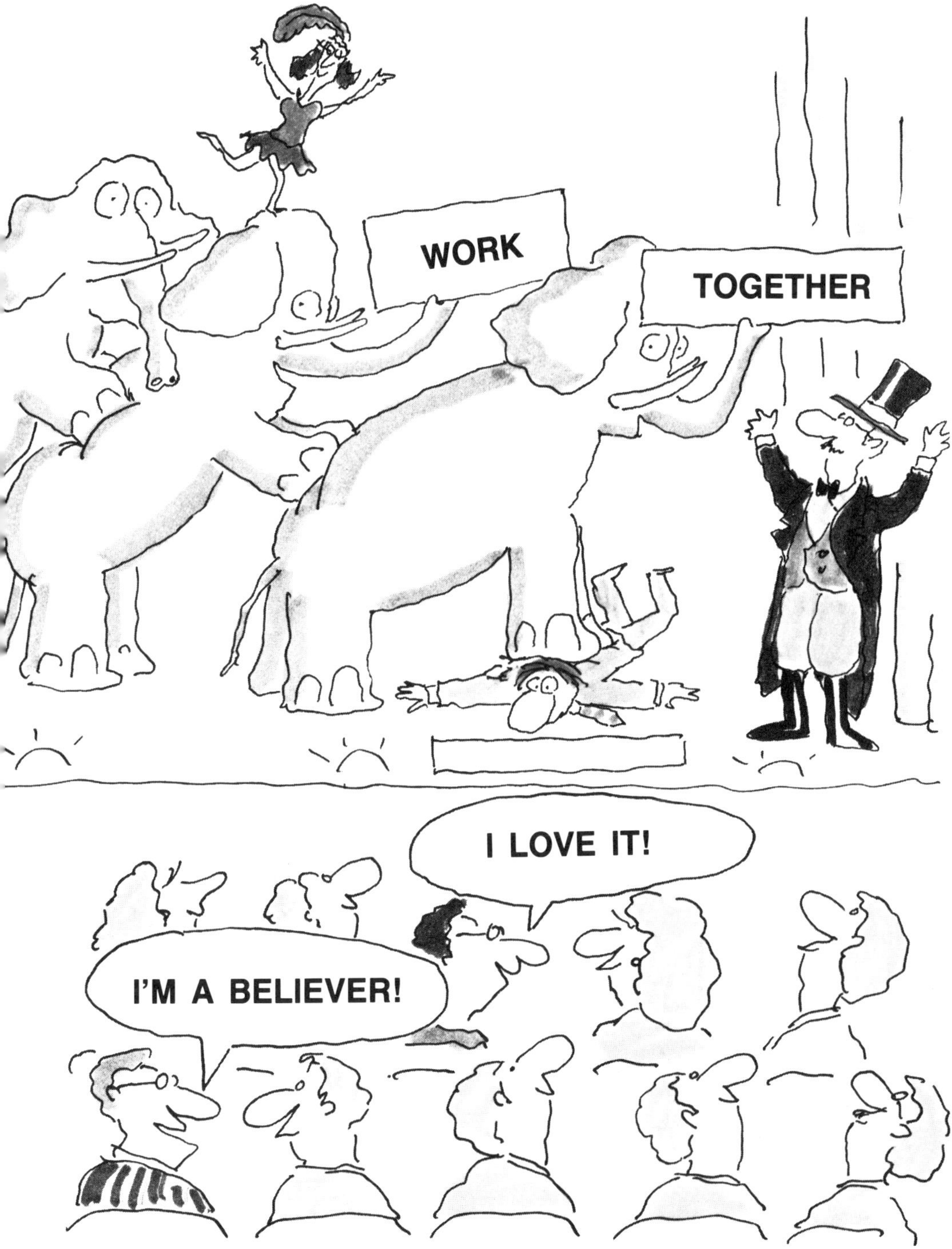

WORK
TOGETHER
I LOVE IT!
I'M A BELIEVER!

Appendix

The effective chairperson's quiz

THE FOLLOWING is a checklist designed to measure your ability to get through a meeting and accomplish <u>absolutely nothing</u>. Have you mastered the art?

		Yes	No
1)	Do you know why you called the meeting?		
2)	Did more than half the attendees manage to stay awake?		
3)	Have you made a decision—any decision?		
4)	Have you followed the agenda?		
5)	Have you set out an objective?		
6)	Has more than an hour passed without a violent argument?		
7)	Did anyone in your audience have a chance to express an opinion?		
8)	Has anyone's idea been accepted?		
9)	Were you successful in bringing the meeting to a close and agreeing on a plan of action?		
10)	Has anyone complained about lack of entertainment?		
11)	Has anyone told you your jokes weren't funny?		
12)	Did anyone—including you—know the purpose of the meeting?		
13)	Did you make any comment that could be called "relevant"?		
14)	Have more than twice as many people shown up at the meeting than was necessary?		

15) Has the thermostat indicated the presence of hot air? ____ ____

16) Have less than three people talked at once at any one time? ____ ____

17) Did you or the group have enough information to solve the problem? ____ ____

18) Has anybody made any sense? ____ ____

If you marked yes to any one of these questions, go back to page one of this book and start all over again.